A
SPIRITUAL
JOURNEY
Through
BREAST
CANCER

A SPIRITUAL JOURNEY *Through* BREAST CANCER

STRENGTH FOR TODAY HOPE FOR TOMORROW

JUDY ASTI

NORTHFIELD PUBLISHING
CHICAGO

ISBN: 1-881273-35-0

3 5 7 9 10 8 6 4 2

Printed in the United States of America

For Pierre
God's man every step of the journey

Do not grieve, for the joy of the LORD is your strength.
—Nehemiah 8:10

CONTENTS

PREFACE

Sometimes on clear nights my husband and I relax after dinner in the swirling warm water of our backyard spa. Sitting there, with the steam rising around me, I look up at the bright stars in the black sky and I sense God's presence. "Lift your eyes and look to the heavens: Who created all these? He who brings out the starry host one by one, and calls them each by name. Because of his great power and mighty strength, not one of them is missing" (Isaiah 40:26).

I heard somewhere that the mathematical probability of this incredible universe actually evolving out of a random explosion is about the same as the chances of an explosion in a print shop causing the dictionary to be written. Even on nights when I can't see any logical pattern in the stars, I still know it was God drawing back His arm and hurling a shower of light into the eternal blackness.

Some people say the whole universe is random because there is no God. I thought about that more than once as I flew through the darkness like a star, aflame and luminous. Suddenly I plummeted, shattered into a billion shards, seemingly a firework whose moment had passed.

Yet for now, at least, my light still shines, and on these nights in the backyard I look up at the stars, see the vastness, feel my own smallness. There is a God, and He knows where I am.

> *I will not die but live,*
>> *and will proclaim what the Lord has done.*
> *The Lord has chastened me severely,*
>> *but he has not given me over to death.*
>> —Psalm 118:17–18

SPECIAL THANKS

The following people saved my life in so many ways:

My faithful family, Olive Ree Robertson, Rick Robertson, Cindi Bunch, Helen and Robert Asti, plus all their clans.

Dan Yeary, who first introduced me to Jesus Christ and encouraged me to write my way through the cancer storm.

My friend J. J. Benkert, who read every draft and cheered me to the finish line.

My special encouragers, Shellie Gay Bohannon, Candy and Dave Yocom, Sue and Basil Marotta.

The members of Bloomfield Hills Baptist Church, leaders of the BSF Bloomfield Hills Evening Women's Class, and saints from coast to coast who ministered to me and prayed for healing.

My brilliant and long-suffering medical team, Dr. Pamela Benitez, Dr. David Decker, Veronica Decker RN, Dr. Ishmael Jaiyesimi, Dr. Gilbert Ladd, Dr. Steven McClelland, Dr. Howard Schwartz, Dr. Daniel Sherbert, Dr. Sheldon Siegel, Dr. JoAnn Smith, and Dr. Jannifer Stromberg.

Michael Briggs, for placing my manuscript into hands I couldn't reach and enduring a million e-mails with grace.

Elsa Mazon and Moody Press, for believing in the project when no other publishers did. Anne Scherich, for her thoughtful editing.

My best friend and devoted husband, Pierre, and my sons, Trevor, Lance, and Truett, who tirelessly poured out their love when I didn't deserve it and gave me a reason to fight the battle.

My Lord and Savior, Jesus Christ, who proved Himself to be everything I hoped He would be and more. All glory to Him.

One

HEAD ON

The seas have lifted up, O LORD,
the seas have lifted up their voice;
the seas have lifted up their pounding waves.
— PSALM 93:3 —

It is summer, 1959. An ink-black sky littered with stars stretches over our little neighborhood in rural Maryland. We children have been summoned home from our evening play and are wearing fresh pajamas, our hair still damp from our baths. The windows of every home are open in hopes of catching a cool night breeze. Crickets serenade. A car occasionally passes by. That's when my dad decides to liven things up by driving a locomotive down our street.

Armed with a new state-of-the-art hi-fi and emboldened by my mother's absence, my father stretches the wires and positions the speakers, complete with the latest in woofers and tweeters, on our front porch. He places a new LP record of sound effects on the turntable. Then he turns up the volume to the highest decibel and sets a train loose to speed through the neighborhood, choo-chooing and woo-wooing like mad down our street.

Our surprised neighbors fly out of their houses in curlers and bathrobes, although the closest railroad tracks are miles away. They stumble into the darkness, trying to make sense of things as my prankster father oversees the scene from our front porch.

Fast-forward forty years. . . . My pastor tells a funny story that ends like this: Just when you think you see the light at the end of the long dark tunnel, it turns out to be the headlights of an on-coming locomotive. I begin to laugh uncontrollably because that's what it was like when I was diagnosed with cancer, and there is a fine line between laughter and tears. The long dark tunnel my hus-band, Pierre, and I had been down was ten years of devastating financial reversal. Finally, we were paying off the last of our bills and seeing what we thought was the light at the end of the tun-nel, better times ahead. That's just when the diagnosis came—ad-vanced breast cancer—like a locomotive coming at us full speed from out of nowhere. Only this time it is my Father in heaven over-seeing the scene, and I am the one stumbling into the darkness trying to make sense of things.

Just before I was diagnosed, I dreamed an unusual dream. In it, I am standing in a charming white gazebo perched on a tiny peninsula made of soft sand. I am nearly surrounded by clear, aqua water that spreads out in a great flat expanse to the edge of the world. Relaxed and warm, the taste of salt on my skin, I lean against the handrail and gaze out over the placid sea and feel the deepest peace I have ever known. I vow to stay here, always.

Suddenly my eye is drawn to the south where a towering tidal wave rears up dark and ominous and approaches fast. I run from the gazebo, frantically searching for something to hold on to when the water slams onto the shore, but I can't find anything. Just as the thundering water is about to crash over my head, I wake up.

I'm not exactly sure why, but I believe this dream is from God.

For one thing, the colors in my dream are unusually vivid. For another, the dream gives me a sense of foreboding I can't shake.

Throughout history God has used dreams to teach or warn his people. Israel's King David writes, "I will praise the LORD, who counsels me; even at night my heart instructs me" (Psalm 16:7). An angel appears to Joseph in a dream and tells him to take Mary and Jesus and flee to Egypt to escape the murderous Herod (Matthew 2:13).

In my case, I think it odd that I dream of approaching calamity just when our family is nearing the end of our financial debacle. As I think about the dream in the following days, it seems to be asking a question: "What will I cling to when the inevitable roar of trouble breaks over me?" My immediate answer is Christ, although I don't know fully what that means.

In real life, of course, I don't wake up in time to avoid the crashing waves of calamity, and I am forced to figure out what I will cling to.

It is a glorious Michigan summer afternoon, and I am a glorious woman in it. I am out of work early and feeling giddy, like a child playing hooky. My car is bathed in golden sunlight; my long skirt hiked up above my knees. I am running late for a doctor's appointment. I drive with my car windows open. Warm, sweet-smelling air swirls around me, messing up my hair, but I don't care. I am a glorious woman in a glorious day.

At the doctor's office, a nurse takes me to a private examination room without a wait. It is that kind of day. Alone, I take off my blouse and put on a flimsy pink paper vest. I sit high up on an examination table covered with white paper and wait for the doctor.

I hear muffled voices outside my door. Dr. Daniel Sherbert enters carrying my file. He is a gentle, tall man with dark brown hair and a bushy brown mustache. He smiles kindly and shakes my hand. He sits down on a stool and rolls close to me. We talk for a minute about the magnificent weather; he examines a small incision on my breast that is healing nicely, then his face changes into a kind of therapeutic blankness. He opens my file and says, "You have cancer."

Cancer. That most dreaded of all words comes at me now out of nowhere, like a baseball hurled toward a pitcher who is looking in another direction, unprotected. *Cancer.* It whacks my face full force, and the sting brings tears to my eyes.

I cannot have cancer. I am a young woman. There must be a mistake. Dr. Sherbert shows me the pathology report. I stare at it and try to focus on his words.

"Lobular," he says, "slow growing. You may have had it a long time. It's more than six centimeters. That's stage three."

Dr. Sherbert is talking, but my head is full of white static. I can't hear. I clutch my paper vest closed in front. "Surgery," he says. "Mastectomy. Chemotherapy. Radiation." They are words with no relationship to me.

The oxygen has been sucked out of the room, and I can't breathe.

"I did everything," I blurt too loudly. "I did everything I was supposed to do."

"It happens sometimes," he says softly.

I think of my husband and my three sons, and tears roll down my cheeks. Dr. Sherbert hands me a Kleenex, his face no longer therapeutically blank. He looks uncomfortable. Bad news is not his specialty.

He pats my knee. "Do you have any questions?"

Questions? Life as I know it, the life I have greeted every morning of my forty-six years, the life in which I live and move and have my being has come to an end, and I don't even know the right questions to ask.

I have cried for so many days that my eyes are swollen nearly shut. I have cancer.

A friend had cancer, too. *Had* cancer; she emphasizes the past tense. A surgeon with a steady hand and a sharp scalpel cut her tumor from her colon. Then they attacked her body with chemotherapy and radiation in case they didn't get all the cells.

She looks frail when I see her on Saturday.

"You're in the worst time," she says, "the very worst time. You know you have cancer, but you don't have a plan."

A plan is what I need—a plan to gather a team of doctors I don't know, to create a treatment program I don't want, to fight an enormous cancer I shouldn't have.

I am like many cancer patients. The very worst time is immediately after the shock of the diagnosis. There are so many unknowns. That is when it is crucial to turn to our omniscient God. He promises to show the way. "This is what the LORD says . . . 'I am the LORD your God, who teaches you what is best for you, who directs you in the way you should go'" (Isaiah 48:17).

I am waiting to see a surgeon, sitting high up on an examination table. I hold the front of my flimsy paper vest shut with one hand and dab at the corners of my eyes with a damp Kleenex to keep my mascara from running. Pierre waits with me, sitting quietly in a chair by the door. He hands me a dry Kleenex.

The surgeon enters, a small man, seemingly not much older than my oldest son. He is wearing a white lab coat.

"Let's have a look," he says. He doesn't notice that I am crying. He examines my breasts in silence, kneading them like bread dough, first one side, then the other.

"Your cancer is extensive," he tells me, as if I didn't already know it. "The other breast appears clear, but if you were my wife or sister I would take both breasts," he says. "That is my recommendation." He is oddly detached as if this is not my body we are talking about.

"What about reconstruction?" I whisper.

"No reconstruction for at least a year," he says flatly. Bad news is this doctor's specialty.

Later I memorize Psalm 139:5–10:

You hem me in—behind and before;

you have laid your hand upon me.

Such knowledge is too wonderful for me,

too lofty for me to attain.

Where can I go from your Spirit?

Where can I flee from your presence?

If I go up to the heavens, you are there;

if I make my bed in the depths, you are there.

If I rise on the wings of the dawn,

if I settle on the far side of the sea,

even there your hand will guide me,

your right hand will hold me fast.

During many of the hard times I will recall it, a comforting reminder of God's presence and control in my life, no matter how things appear at the time.

On this day, however, Pierre drives home with one hand, holds my hand tightly with his other. We don't speak a word about the surgeon's unspeakable recommendation.

When I get home I go straight upstairs to our bed and cry into a Kleenex, just tears at first, then escalating sobs. Pierre sits down beside me and wraps his arms around the knot of my body. He holds me tight as we sit on our bed crying and rocking.

"We've been through tough times before. We can do this together," he whispers. "You can make it."

It will be weeks before I stop crying. And, although he tries, Pierre can't keep me together, for it is the Lord Himself who holds us together when life feels like it is tearing apart at the seams. "He is before all things, and in him all things hold together" (Colossians 1:17).

I have not yet turned to Him.

☒　　☒　　☒

I read somewhere that babies without fathers have a higher incidence of hearing problems because, when a father tosses a baby up in the air and catches it, somehow the jostling helps develop the baby's ears.

I wake up at 5:30 A.M., and that one sentence is on my mind. I think about hearing God because I have never needed to hear Him as badly as I need to hear Him now. I ask Him what it means to hold on to Christ, to trust Him when it seems impossible for Him to do anything. To abide. I don't know what it means to abide, so I look it up. Abide: to wait for, to endure without yielding, to bear patiently, to accept without objection. I think about those definitions and write my own version: *To endure hardship without losing hope.*

Exactly what is it we hope for? That we will not have to endure hardship?

It is too late for me. I have cancer. Hardship is washing over me and not for the first time. Can I dare to hope that I will endure it without crumbling? Can I hope that the gospel is true, that there is another life beyond this life where all wrongs are made right and every tear wiped dry? That cancer is not the last word?

"Remember," my friend says, "cancer starts with a lower case c; Christ starts with a capital."

For nearly twenty-five years I have said that I trust Christ, but now, in the biggest crisis of my life, can I? I have a decision to make. Either I will trust Christ to guide me through cancer, or I will not. This is in many ways an intellectual decision based on what I know the Bible says and what I have experienced so far in my life.

I am driving in my car when I decide. Stopped at a traffic signal, I watch the light change from red to green, and in my mind I give Christ the green light, too. It is that simple. No matter what happens, I will trust Christ and I will not turn back. It is a decision I will have to keep making daily.

Christ, the Good Shepherd, leads His sheep away from the dangers they wander into; protects the sheep from the dangers that wander into them. His sheep follow Him because they know His voice.

"The watchman opens the gate for him, and the sheep listen to his voice. He calls his own sheep by name and leads them out. When he has brought out all his own, he goes on ahead of them, and his sheep follow him because they know his voice" (John 10:3–4).

My Father in heaven throws me up seemingly out of His grasp, and, like a baby, maybe the jostling will develop my ears a little and I will hear Him whisper, *"Come, follow Me."*

JOURNEY SURVIVAL GUIDE

A cancer diagnosis is nearly always a devastating shock. However, today it is far from an automatic death sentence. No one wants to have cancer, but we should all be encouraged by the hundreds of thousands of survivor success stories. There is always hope. Best of all, our God can be trusted, even with cancer. He is present with His children no matter what comes our way. And, as I later discovered, cancer is an exhilarating journey with God, like no other. Today, when nonbelievers tell me Jesus is just a crutch, I answer them, "Crutch? He's a whole hospital."

When you pass through the waters,
I will be with you;
and when you pass through the rivers,
they will not sweep over you.
Isaiah 43:2

Two

HOWARD BE THY NAME

Fear the LORD, you his saints,
for those who fear him lack nothing.
—◦ PSALM 34:9 ◦—

I am driving home from work trying to decide which musical version of the Twenty-third Psalm I want to open my funeral with. I think the psalm usually comes near the end, but I want to open with it to get off to a dramatic start.

Kathy Troccoli has a new rendition that is bordering on exotic, with her deep, husky voice and instruments that sound as if they might have been shipped from the rain forest. I cue it up on my CD player. She is singing two things simultaneously that make the hair stand up on my arms because I am, myself, caught in a dichotomy, simultaneously allowing myself to wallow in self-pity and wanting to draw closer to God.

I pencil in *Kathy Troccoli* in the spiral notebook balanced on my thigh and steer around the minivan stopped in front of me for a left turn.

Closed casket!!! I write that down, adding the exclamation marks. Nobody would ever get my hair and makeup right.

It is a warm summer evening. I drive with the windows open thinking about my life and what I have to show for it. I think of my three sons. They are what I have to show for my life. I think of the godly young men they are turning out to be. I skip a line in the notebook. *Make sure the boys have suits that fit.*

I want my funeral to be a statement of a life lived for Jesus. I make a list of the friends I want to have speak. No, they should read Scripture, or they might say something that would put the attention on me instead of Jesus. Still, it will be emotional for some. My own eyes get teary just thinking about it.

I eject Kathy Troccoli and shove in Twila Paris's *Sanctuary* CD. I decide to end with "Let Them Praise." This would bring the funeral to a close with all the attention on Jesus instead of me.

It doesn't occur to me that even as I am planning for all the attention to be on Jesus, my motivation is to make myself look good one last time for doing it. It is a common practice, however; planning your own funeral when you have treatable cancer may be an attempt to be in control even after you are dead.

X   X   X

Pierre goes into his office early. He calls his friend and personal physician Howard Schwartz, a loquacious Jewish man with a big heart.

Howard is not in his office when Pierre calls him.

"It's a personal emergency," Pierre informs his receptionist. She assures him that Howard will call from his cell phone.

Within minutes Pierre's phone rings.

"Guess where I am," Howard shouts into the phone.

"Tell me!" Pierre is not in the mood for games.

"I'm walking down Fifth Avenue. Can you believe it? I'm in New York on Fifth Avenue right now. What's going on?"

"It's Judy," Pierre says. "She has cancer."

"She's had a positive biopsy?"

"Yes. They say it's really bad. I don't know what to do."

"How bad?"

"Stage three."

"Oh no."

"Howard, I'm totally out of my element. Judy is planning her funeral. We're both numb. We don't know what to do."

"Hold on a second," Howard says. "Did I tell you I'm on Fifth Avenue? Hold on a second." He partially covers the mouthpiece of his phone with his hand and shouts to the city of New York, "Would you be quiet? I'm a doctor, and I've got a patient I can't hear."

"OK," he says. "I'm ducking into a quiet place. Cancer. OK, I'll tell you what, don't worry, do you hear me? Don't worry. I'm in New York on Fifth Avenue, it's Friday, but I'm flying home Sunday afternoon. Don't worry; this is my element. I know everyone. Do you hear me? I know everyone. Doctors take care of each other, so from now on consider yourselves Dr. and Mrs. Asti. I'll come straight to your house from the airport. I'm getting in at one o'clock. Don't worry about anything. I'll come straight to your house, and you can tell me what's going on. Don't worry. I'll take care of everything."

On Saturday I lie out by the swimming pool in our backyard. All the boys are at work, so I wear a small purple bikini, Pierre's favorite. Today I feel exceedingly sorry for myself, and this suit seems like the perfect torture for me because, when the doctors get finished with me, I probably will never be able to wear it again. Perhaps no woman my age should even think of wearing it, but why should I care what a forty-six year old woman should be wearing? I decide right then and there with the sun baking my body that

I'm through playing by the rules. I am going to stop using sun block, start eating all the grease and chocolate I want, and drive fast. All my life I have played by the rules, and now I am dying of cancer. No fair.

In my self-pity I forget that God is in control of our lives . . . and our deaths. Cancer does not take Him by surprise. Although I might ultimately die of cancer, it won't be one day before the Lord has planned. "All the days ordained for me were written in your book before one of them came to be" (Psalm 139:16). Considering your own mortality is healthy. Dwelling on it is destructive.

On Sunday afternoon Howard rings our doorbell, still dressed in his traveling clothes. It is a warm, sunny day. We move out to our patio overlooking the pool, out of earshot of our sons. For the first time since I have known Howard, he stops talking completely while I tell him my story. He listens in earnest silence as I tell him I did everything I was supposed to do. For four years I showed a lump to a doctor who assured me it was ordinary breast tissue. Nothing conclusive showed up in the mammogram. Now the biopsy report shows I'm stage three.

"It's not fair," I say. "Life was just opening up to us." I have held up well, but now, having stated what I see to be the truth—a future that looked infinitely brighter than our recent past is about to be stolen from us—I start to cry.

Howard hands me a Kleenex to dab at my eyes. "You'll get an eye infection from that mascara," he says. He smiles as only Howard smiles, eyebrows raised, the corners of his mouth turned up slightly.

Then he gets serious and talks fast. "OK," he says. "First, nobody said life was fair. There are no guarantees for any of us. I might walk out to my car and get hit by a truck. Second, you have the wrong doctors, and I can get you in with the right doctors.

I'm going to call David Decker. He's the oncologist I want you with. And I'm going to call him at home today. Don't worry about anything. I'm going to oversee your case. You'll have the best of care, the best doctors. Remember, you are Dr. and Mrs. Asti. I'm not a cancer doctor, but I had cancer."

This takes me by surprise. Looking at Howard, glowing with health, it's hard to believe he has had cancer.

"A melanoma on my leg," he says, "a spot as small as the point of a ballpoint pen. The doctor told me I could watch it. 'Watch it?' I said. 'Why would I want to watch it? You watch it. Put it in a jar of formaldehyde and sit it on your desk and watch it if you want.' They took out a piece of my leg the size of a baseball to make sure they got it all. 'Watch it,' he said. When a patient of mine tells me she has a lump in her breast that the gynecologist is watching, I tell her, 'Watch it in a jar of formaldehyde. That's where breast lumps belong.'

"Believe me," he says, "the word *cancer* will never be the same to you. But you can do this. Don't worry about anything. I'll oversee your case. You need the right doctors, and Howard Schwartz can get you in where you can't get in. Do you understand? There are doctors you can't get in to see in this decade, but I will get you in."

An hour after leaving our home, Howard calls me. "I've talked to David Decker. Call his office tomorrow, and he'll come in early any day to see you. And here's his home number in case you want to talk to him before then."

I am having tests all day at Howard's orders, including a bone scan, a bone survey, a chest X-ray, and a brain CT Scan. Pierre takes the day off, so I dress up for it. It's a hot summer day. I wear a fuchsia dress with a tank top that reveals my tan shoulders and a sarong skirt that opens a little when I walk. Maybe I'll never look great to Pierre again.

All day, in various venues, Pierre sits calmly with me while my blood is drawn and nuclear medicine is injected into my veins. He can't come with me where the machines work, so I lie alone, except for the presence of preoccupied technicians, on robotic tables, while high-tech cameras take pictures of the inside of my body, searching for hidden tumors that might be lurking like muggers in dark alleys.

My brain CT scan is scheduled for 9:00 P.M. A nurse takes five pokes on the inside of my arm to access a vein, leaving a wicked bruise that will take weeks to disappear. I lie on a table that glides me into the cylindrical CT scan machine. It is there, where I have to be perfectly still while they take pictures of my brain, that the tears start to come, running out the sides of my eyes and filling up my ears.

When the CT scan ends, I start sobbing. A young female technician in purple scrubs asks if they said or did anything wrong. I shake my head. She puts her hand on my shoulder, "Just the whole thing; we understand."

But they don't understand. Nobody who has not had cancer will ever understand.

✗   ✗   ✗

Putting together the right team of doctors is crucial to survival. In most cases it is fine to take a week or two to interview doctors. There are many good doctors associated with most insurance companies, free screenings and clinics available, and more than one opinion on treatment options. It's your body. Ask God to lead you to His team of doctors and the treatment plan best for you. Then trust the doctors and the plan. This is vital for maximum results. Select the very best you can and, if possible, choose doctors you like—you will be spending a lot of time with them.

Dr. Decker's waiting room overflows with patients in all stages of cancer. Some look completely normal; some are entirely bald, ashen, and appear so close to death that I can't look at them because I am so afraid that is my destiny, too.

A nurse leads Pierre and me to a small examination room. We don't know what to expect. Dr. Decker enters the room, a thin, balding man wearing a white coat, dark pants, and polished loafers. He has soft blue eyes behind gold-rimmed glasses and a slightly quirky manner that I immediately like because I am slightly quirky myself.

"I'm David Decker," he says. His voice is warm and, although he is quite famous in our city for his breast cancer work, noticeably lacking in arrogance. I like the fact that he meets me fully dressed before he has me change to be examined.

One of the first things I notice about Dr. Decker's practice is the gowns. Before he leaves the room he hands me an immaculate white gown made of real cotton fabric that feels luxurious compared to the flimsy paper vests that have become standard fare for women. It immediately tells me that he respects his patients. The second thing I notice when he returns is the breast exam itself. I have always cringed having to bare my breasts for anyone other than my husband. However, there is something about Dr. Decker's manner, his thorough examination, yet the way he keeps me covered up as much as possible, that allows me to relax in his presence.

Later, seated in his office, Dr. Decker explains my cancer, using drawings and pamphlets to help me understand. He is patient with my questions and in no hurry, as if I am his only concern and his waiting room is not full. He explains that his role as the oncologist is the administration of chemotherapy, but my cancer will require a team of doctors in addition to an oncologist: a breast surgeon, a radiation oncologist, and, if I choose, a plastic surgeon.

"I don't know why you were told to take both breasts," he says. "The odds are higher that a recurrence would be in an organ. But with Adriamycin and Cytoxan, your chances improve dramatically. Then radiation lowers the chances of recurrence even further, and if surgery suggests another round of chemotherapy, that will be

Taxol, which lowers your chances for recurrence even more. We follow up by putting you on Tamoxifin for five years.

"I wish I could say that eliminates your chances for recurrence, but really your chances of a recurrence are actually lower than the chances of somebody on the street getting cancer for the first time. I don't make the decision about surgery. You'll meet with each member of the team, and then we'll work together to determine the course of treatment. Let's get you in with the right breast surgeon and see what they have to say."

He picks up the phone to call the surgeon himself.

He has told me too much to absorb in a world that is out of control. However, Pierre is making notes. It is a good idea to take someone with you any time you will be receiving information. When you are upset, you simply can't remember it all.

I look around Dr. Decker's office and notice he has a prayer hanging on the wall. He is on hold.

"I understand that you're confused, scared, and mad," he says. "But, Judy, your chances of survival are excellent. I think you should go into this with a positive attitude." I can already feel my attitude changing. Being in Dr. Decker's presence feels like a safe harbor from a raging storm.

X   X   X

Dr. Pamela Benitez is the breast surgeon. Dr. Decker has asked her to see me quickly as a personal favor to him, but she is booked solid for weeks. My friends start praying that Dr. Benitez will work me in quickly. She does.

Her waiting room is small. Pierre and I sit side by side in cushioned chairs. The other women waiting swap war stories. What kind of surgery they had. Which breast. I study the open magazine in my lap with great intensity. I am in no mood to talk to strangers about my breasts.

A nurse escorts us to a private examination room. Dr. Benitez enters with my file and firmly tells Pierre, who is standing, to sit in a chair. She is a young, attractive, slightly Latin-looking woman, fairly small in stature but definitely in charge. She inserts my mammogram films into the frame of a light box and studies them. She leaves the room while I change, then examines my breasts while I lie down. She has me sit up and examines me with my arms in the air, then with my arms akimbo.

I start talking fast about everything we have learned from our research about new treatments that can reduce surgery—preceding the surgery with chemotherapy to reduce the tumor and then opting for a lumpectomy. I am determined to keep my breast. Pierre can remember the right terminology, and he uses it. He discusses Sentinel Node Biopsy to reduce the removal of lymph nodes.

"I have to be able to wear a bathing suit." I am back to saving my breast. "We are a family of swimmers. We *live* in our bathing suits in the summer."

Dr. Benitez listens patiently, then says softly, "I understand your desire to save your breast." Then she delivers the news I don't want to hear. "With cancer this advanced, if I am the surgeon, there can be nothing less than a mastectomy on the one breast. My job is to save your life."

Although I already know that the cancer I have is life threatening, hearing her say this hits me hard. I have been planning my funeral but always in a vague state of unreality. Now the truth that I might actually lose my life is real.

"What about reconstruction?" I whisper.

"Absolutely," she says. "The plastic surgeon can work with me during the surgery. This is being done more and more frequently with good success." She hugs me warmly. "You can do this," she says. A button on her white coat says "I (heart) a survivor." A gold cross gleams against her breastbone.

33

When we arrive at the office of Dr. Jannifer Stromberg, the radiation oncologist recommended by Dr. Decker, a nurse takes us to a private examination room and confesses she doesn't know where the doctor is. A young Asian resident with a heavy accent enters and informs us that he will take all the information. I tell him my whole story, not realizing that I will have to repeat it to the doctor. He is just practicing getting the facts, but I am too new to hospital protocol to realize I am helping with his education.

I am annoyed by the time Dr. Stromberg is finally summoned. But when she walks into the room she immediately disarms me with her warmth, sincere apologies, and lack of conceit. She is a pretty blonde woman in her mid-thirties. She tells me a patient in serious trouble needed her in the hospital, and I admit to myself that I want a doctor like that.

"Radiation follows the mastectomy," she says matter-of-factly.

I immediately start crying.

Dr. Stromberg is mortified. "I'm sorry, I shouldn't have assumed mastectomy; it's just with cancer this advanced . . ." She pulls several Kleenex from a box and hands them to me.

"Let's wait until Dr. Decker, Dr. Benitez, and I have talked about the appropriate course of treatment before we make any assumptions," she says. Her eyes are watery.

My worst fears are confirmed when the three doctors confer. Mastectomy is inevitable, although it will be preceded by three months of chemotherapy in hopes of shrinking the mass so that surgery will produce clean margins, meaning that the outermost tissue that is removed doesn't reveal any cancer cells, which otherwise could already have metastasized, or moved, into the rest of my body.

My phone rings after dinner. "How did you like Decker?" It is Howard.

"He's great, and so are the other doctors he recommended."

"I told you I'd take care of you. Didn't I tell you I'd take care of you? I am *going* to take care of you. I've gotten all the results of your tests. I had all the test results sent to me. They are all negative. There is no evidence of cancer anywhere else. Not in your bones or your brain. Your tests are all negative. This is good news. This is very good news."

"Thank you, Howard. You're a true friend."

"Don't worry about anything. Howard Schwartz will be looking over all the doctors' shoulders. I'll take care of you."

A crisis like cancer helps you quickly sort your friends into three categories: those who do, those who encourage, and those who forget they know you. Howard is a doer.

"Don't worry. I'm in this for the long haul," he says. "I'll take care of you."

✶   ✶   ✶

Before treatments even start, cancer changes everything about my life. There is hardly a moment of any day, or of my sleepless nights, when I am not focused on it.

I am a "why" person, and my prayer life has become the repeated questions, "Why me, God? Why now, God?" In the most brilliant move of my life I married Pierre, a "how" person: "How, God? Show us." I begin reading books on cancer and quickly learn that moving from groveling in the why arena to taking the initiative in the how arena could save my life.

As I search my Bible for answers over the next few weeks, God shows me something interesting: His people. This is what I discovered: Ordinarily, God's people live extraordinary lives. In my search of the Bible, I don't find any ordinary lives. For God has found worthy of record the lives of ordinary people who did extraordinary things. Big things and small things.

Abraham walks up Mt. Moriah with fire in his hand, a knife in his belt, and a churning in his stomach, to sacrifice his son Isaac on the altar they will build themselves. The young Rebekah leaves

35

her family and her country and travels nearly six hundred miles to marry a man she has never seen. Moses leads more than a million Israelites out of Egypt only to discover Pharaoh's army is in hot pursuit and the Red Sea blocks the way. Joshua instructs the Israelites to conquer Jericho by marching around it and blowing their horns. A small group of unimpressive Jews leaves everything to follow a stranger named Jesus, who makes the preposterous claim to be God Himself.

These are ordinary people who do extraordinary things because they believe it is God asking them to do it.

On the way up the mountain, Abraham makes conversation with Isaac, but his voice is strained with grief. He doesn't know about the ram waiting in the thicket for the sacrifice. Rebekah takes her chances like a mail-order bride and becomes a mother in the line of the promised seed of Christ. Moses is sweating bullets as Pharaoh's army bears down when suddenly the Red Sea divides, walls of water miraculously held back on either side of them, forming a dry corridor for their passage to safety. Joshua surely feels foolish telling the people to blow their horns and shout, yet suddenly the walls of Jericho collapse and they take the city. The disciples hide in the shadows while their Jesus-God is crucified, but after His resurrection they find their own lives resurrected as well.

God asks us to trust Him without our knowing what He has up His sleeve.

Yet we know we have an extraordinary God. By the word of His mouth He brought the entire universe into being. By His Word He brings us from darkness into light.

He still works in extraordinary ways. For me, a depressed, scared-to-death cancer patient, God asks that I simply trust Him. Then He uses a make-it-happen Jewish doctor named Howard Schwartz to start the ball rolling to put together a team of physicians who will be God's divine agents in a life-or-death battle for physical, emotional, and spiritual healing.

JOURNEY SURVIVAL GUIDE

God often provides in surprising ways. Ravens fed Elijah (1 Kings 17:2–6). An angel instructed Philip to leave a successful revival to go answer the questions of an Ethiopian eunuch, one man searching for truth (Acts 8:26–39). And Jesus fed more than five thousand people with five loaves of bread and two fish (Matthew 14:13–21). Jehovah Jireh, God Our Provider, is often listed as one of the Lord's names. In a crisis like cancer it is important to remember that if we trust God, He will provide everything we need, exactly when we need it. He has resources we aren't aware of, yet He doesn't necessarily reveal in advance what He plans to do. That is where our faith comes in. The Scriptures repeatedly show us we can trust Him to provide.

> *Abraham looked up and there in a thicket he saw a ram caught by its horns. He went over and took the ram and sacrificed it as a burnt offering instead of his son. So Abraham called that place "The LORD will provide." And to this day it is said, "On the mountain of the LORD it will be provided."*
>
> Genesis 22:13–14

A NIGHT TO REMEMBER

Whether you turn to the right or to the left,
your ears will hear a voice behind you, saying,
"This is the way; walk in it."

—◦ ISAIAH 30:21 ◦—

The diagnosis of cancer is accompanied by its own unique breed of attendant terrors. For the Christian who knows the Bible's teaching about the future, death is not the ultimate fear. Death is a doorway into an eternity of joy, of life in a new and glorified state, of seeing Jesus face to face. Still, death brings separation from loved ones, which, for a wife and mother like me, is a genuine cause for anxiety, for how will my family manage without me?

We forget that even our families belong to God and that He is capable of handling the situation. Although thoughts of my own mortality are always present now, as I begin the cancer journey, there is another fear that looms even larger and more terrifying, and that is what the disease will be permitted to do to me as it runs its course, before I am ushered, at last, through the doorway to glory.

⚸   ⚸   ⚸

We have to tell the boys I have cancer. Pierre and I pray together that we will not show fear or break down. We carefully plan to gather the three of them in our bedroom tonight and tell them.

They have been out together for the evening, and we hear them laughing when they get home. Their steps are heavy as they come up the stairs in their big men's bodies. We call them into our bedroom. Pierre and I sit on our bed, propped against the pillows. Trevor drapes himself stomach down across the end of our bed. Lance and Truett sit together on the striped chaise nearby, jostling for the most comfortable position.

"We have something serious to talk about," Pierre says. "We need your full attention." The seriousness of his voice gets their attention.

"We're not moving again, are we?" Truett asks.

"No." Pierre pauses, thinking of exactly how to put it, and he quietly says, "Mom has been diagnosed with breast cancer."

The boys are silent, their faces softly illuminated in the lamplight.

Pierre says evenly, "We have seen a variety of doctors, and we have chosen excellent ones. A course of treatment will start soon. We don't want you to be worried. The doctors are very encouraging. But it's a battle we need to fight together."

The boys sit unusually still.

Then Trevor, a pre-med student, wants to know more. "What stage?"

"Three."

"What treatment?"

"Chemo . . . mastectomy . . . radiation . . . maybe more chemo."

Trevor is quiet.

"We need to pull together as a family," I say. "I need your support to get through this."

The boys look at each other for clues. They have never been told before that their mother has cancer. They don't know how to respond.

"Don't worry," I say. "The doctors will put me back together as good as new. I'm going to get reconstructive surgery so I won't look weird in a bathing suit."

"Are you going to get big ones?" somebody asks.

"No."

"Shoot."

We all laugh. Then Lance and Truett move over to our bed. The boys each tenderly kiss and hug me, and the five of us sit in a circle, our heads bowed inward, huddled on the bed in the lamplight, a team leaning in to discuss the game plan.

X   X   X

I am talking to my friend JoAnne Hazel before our Sunday morning Bible study begins. She is a tall Texan, one of the few women I know who is taller than I, and we talk eye to eye. She knows about my cancer.

"You shouldn't have this," she says. "You're too young. It's not fair."

I feel sorry for myself today. She's right, it isn't fair, and I mumble, "I have hell ahead." Then, as I lower my body into my chair, I clearly hear God speak to me as close to audibly as I have ever heard Him. He says, "No, Judy, it's heaven ahead."

I know that throughout history God has spoken in a variety of ways. He spoke through His prophets. He speaks through Scripture. He speaks in dreams. He speaks through His people. Once He even spoke through a donkey (Numbers 22:27–31). God also speaks through our circumstances. And sometimes He speaks to us directly, as he has occasionally done in my own life, almost but not quite audibly.

Is it God speaking to me when I hear a voice telling me at the beginning of my cancer battle that it is heaven ahead? I have no other explanation.

Fighting cancer is like running a marathon where all your friends run ahead without you and the batteries in your Walkman go dead. It's a long race, there are too many people you don't know involved, and the usual resources you normally depend on are nowhere to be found.

For me the starting line is a small surgery to install an intravenous port to receive the chemotherapy drip, which is to be the first stage of my treatment. I should be happy about this port that will stop the nurses from poking me repeatedly with needles and will prevent the chemotherapy from spilling into my arm, leaving permanent black burns.

Instead, I am filled with dread.

Pierre waits in a tiny room supplied with padded chairs and magazines. I walk with a hospital escort who is wearing green scrubs into the operating room where I change behind a screen into a hospital gown.

It is a short surgery to install the port in my left arm. The doctor will send a tiny tube from the port through my veins all the way to my heart so that the chemotherapy drugs are immediately distributed into my bloodstream. I lie on a table, surrounded by high-tech machinery and busy technicians. I ask about the screen that looks like a television near my head. A nurse tells me they will use it to watch the tube move through my body.

"Don't worry," she says. "It's a simple procedure. We do a lot of these."

My confidence in the team is short-lived when they scrub my right arm in preparation instead of my left. I refuse the IV until they prepare the correct arm and until the doctor confirms what he is about to do. Apparently this makes me a troublemaker, because the nurses and technicians turn cool toward me.

No matter how excellent, doctors and their staff are imperfect human beings. They make mistakes. Cancer patients and their families must be aware of what is taking place at all times. Every patient may question any procedure scheduled for her own body, even as it is about to begin. Do not allow drugs that induce drowsiness to be administered until you have seen your doctor face to face and discussed what is about to occur. If possible, have the doctor mark the surgery site with a felt-tipped pen. If the patient is too sick, a family member or close friend should step in as the patient's advocate.

The doctor enters the room in his scrubs and confirms the procedure he is about to perform. There is an edge to his voice. Then he straps my left arm into an uncomfortable position, and a nurse swabs it with an orange solution. The "light sleep" they are supposed to put me under turns out to be almost no sleep at all. There is no pain, and nothing unprofessional is said. Still, I am afraid, not because of this surgery but because of the long battle that lies ahead—nearly a year of days like this, a year of my life spent doing little besides fighting cancer and no guarantees at the end of it. For most of the surgery, I use my free hand to dry the tears that burn my face.

When the surgery is over, I dress behind the screen and a hospital escort returns me to Pierre, who is visibly surprised that I am visibly upset by this simple procedure.

Dr. Decker will administer the first chemotherapy that same day. Pierre and I sit nervously in his crowded waiting room. A technician calls my name. She wants a blood sample. She jabs my middle finger and squeezes it to fill a small tube with blood, places a round Band-Aid over the hole in my finger. Then I return to sit beside Pierre. Within minutes, a nurse calls us to a private examination room.

I sit high up on a table lined with white paper. My confidence in what I am about to undergo increases when Dr. Decker enters the room. He examines me and examines the new port about the size of a thimble that juts out of my thin arm on the underside above my elbow. He puts his arm around my shoulders. "Are you ready for this?" he asks, looking at me over his gold-rimmed glasses.

"Do I have a choice?"

"You always have a choice."

"Let's get it over with."

I re-dress, and a pretty blonde nurse takes us to the chemotherapy room, a large, light-filled room lined with about a dozen brown vinyl-covered lounge chairs. Patients with their feet propped up occupy most of the chairs, hooked up to plastic bags hanging from tall stainless steel poles. The bags drip into ports in the patients' arms or on their chests or directly into their veins. There are two televisions in the room showing different shows. Some patients watch TV, some read, some sleep. I carry my son's Discman to listen to while the drugs enter my body.

The nurse shows me to a lounge chair and hands me a pillow and a multicolored crocheted afghan. She offers Pierre a straight-back chair nearby, then leaves to prepare the drugs. She returns with a tray containing several clear bags of liquid and places them on a small tray that extends from the left side of my chair. She asks about my family. She doesn't rush. She has a son, too, she tells me. She patiently explains everything she is about to do. The first bags contain drugs to combat the inevitable nausea caused by the chemotherapy drugs. She easily inserts the needle into my new port with the first try. She unhooks a clamp at the bottom of the bag. The medicine drips into the clear tubing that leads to my port.

Within minutes I am drowsy and cold. I spread the afghan over me and pull it up to my chin. I put on my headphones and listen to a CD to keep my mind off the drugs, which are a kind of poison to every cell in my body. I drift off to sleep.

It is a good idea to take some things with you to chemotherapy to distract your thoughts. Many oncologists have televisions. Some patients can read. Some pray. I couldn't do either, so I always fell asleep to classical music. Be prepared. Some kinds of chemo take hours.

I am only vaguely aware of the nurse adding the more toxic bags of liquid. I am lost in the reverie of drugs and Bach. For four hours the drugs drip. Pierre patiently waits, sitting quietly in his chair.

When all the bags are empty, the nurse removes the needle. Pierre holds my elbow as I walk out to the car on wobbly legs. I feel as if my body has been turned inside out, exposing all my nerve endings.

At home, I go straight to bed. It is Monday night.

Surprisingly on Tuesday morning I feel well enough to go to the advertising agency where I work. I take the prescription drug Zofran to keep the nausea away. It makes me drowsy, but drowsy is better than nauseated. At work I write a few ads and focus on some proofreading. I put in my eight hours, impressing everyone there, including myself, by feeling pretty human.

On Wednesday I go to work again, but this time a state of something less than human comes over me. It is nausea and worse, a feeling like nothing I have ever experienced before. At 10:00 A.M. I call Pierre.

"I'm not going to make it," I say.

"Don't drive home," he says. "I'm on my way."

While I wait for Pierre, I attend a Creative Meeting where everyone who will be involved is discussing a new project. I sit at the conference table with the account executive, the artists, and the agency's owners. Our job is to create the image plus all the ads and collateral sales materials to make the project successful. I know the chairman is annoyed that I am leaving early, but he doesn't say it.

During the meeting, people toss ideas around like Frisbees, but I hear nothing that is said and say nothing myself. As the copy-writing director, I should be coming up with cool ideas. Instead, white static fills my head. My stomach churns. Everyone takes notes while the chairman talks, except me. Files, papers, and coffee cups are scattered over the mahogany conference table. I hold myself very still, afraid I will cover the busy scene with projectile vomit while my coworkers look on in horror.

⚹   ⚹   ⚹

For the next two days I take more serious antinausea drugs and mostly sleep. By the end of the week I feel almost normal again.

The five of us sit at the dinner table.

"I'm over the worst of the first treatment," I say, trying hard to keep my voice cheerful, "except my hair could start falling out soon. Don't worry; I'll have a good wig." Tears fall onto my dinner plate anyway.

Trevor quickly and deliberately stands up. He places his hands on the table, and there is a look on his face bordering on fierceness that I've seen only a few times in the past when, as the captain of the high school baseball team, it was his job to rally the team. "I've been thinking about this," he says. "Our family has been through a lot already. God has never let us down before, and He won't this time."

We finish our dinner with talk about other topics—the flowers in the backyard, the day's events at the pool where the boys work. The determined look stays on Trevor's face. If it's up to him, he will get me through this with sheer will.

⚹   ⚹   ⚹

The weekend following chemotherapy is the weekend Lance goes back to school at the University of Tennessee. I insist on going. I want to do what a normal mother should be doing—taking her son to college. Pierre drives, and I ride most of the eight hours trying not to look out the window at the passing landscape. It brings the nausea back.

Late in the afternoon we park in the crowded lot in front of Lance's dormitory. We load his belongings on a cart and roll it into the elevator, where we ride up to the ninth floor. I am not much help. But at least I am there like a regular mother. I am not just a woman with cancer. I help make his bed and then lie down on it and sleep until it's time to go eat. After dinner, when I kiss Lance good-bye in front of his dormitory, he hugs me long and hard, nearly crushing me with his strong upper body. But there is a quiver in his voice. His eyes are wet. He doesn't want to be away from home when I need help.

"Don't worry," I say. "God will take care of us all."

✗   ✗   ✗

Fourteen days after my first chemotherapy, Dr. Decker's nurse checks my blood to see if the toxins are working. They are, too well. My white blood count is so low it is almost nonexistent. She warns me to stay away from people.

On day fifteen I wake up with a fever and a sore throat. I call in to work sick.

"Go to work," I tell Pierre. "If the fever goes up, I'll call the doctor."

By afternoon the fever is over 101 degrees, and I call.

"We are jammed," the receptionist says. "There is no way Dr. Decker can see you, but come in; Dr. Jaiyesimi will see you."

It is late afternoon. Dr. Decker stands in the hallway as a nurse leads me into an examination room. He looks me up and down over his glasses, has quiet words with Dr. Ishmael Jaiyesimi.

Known as Dr. J to everyone in the office, the doctor is a very tall, very dark African-American man with his head shaved as clean as his cancer patients and a huge smile of white teeth. Raised in Nigeria, he speaks with a heavy accent, and I have a hard time understanding him as he examines me. He pronounces his name for me twice so I can say it right.

"Dat is why I am Dr. J," he says. "I tink you must go to de hosepeetal. You need de antibeeotiks."

"I can take antibiotics at home."

47

"No," he says. "Your eemmune seestem is sooo very weak. You need de IV antibeeotiks. You will only be der a few days."

"A few days?" I blurt loudly. "I can't go to the hospital for days."

"I tink you must. You are very pale. Tings could get sooo seerious."

Dr. J leaves the room, and Dr. Decker, too busy to see me, enters wearing his white coat. He leans back against the windowsill, arms crossed. "Blame me," he says, looking over his glasses. "You need to go. Typically, you'll be there three or four days until your fever is gone and your system is stronger; then you'll go home. Dr. J is on hospital duty. He'll oversee you."

I want Dr. Decker to oversee me. He is my doctor.

Dr. J is standing in the corridor as we walk out of the examination room. "May Gawd be wid you," he says.

There are no beds available at the hospital. A nurse escorts us to Emergency, where they will start the IV antibiotics while we wait for a room.

People crowd the Emergency waiting room. At the admittance desk I explain that I am Dr. Decker's cancer patient in need of antibiotics. I tell the details of my case to four different people, some probably practicing taking the story for their education, but I am so weak I do whatever they tell me. I don't want to be viewed as a troublemaker. A nurse takes us to a private room, where Pierre helps me change into a hospital gown and I lie on a gurney with the back permanently propped into an uncomfortable angle.

"Man," Pierre says. "Did you see all those people sitting out there? How did we get in here so fast?"

"Cancer has a few perks." My grin is weak. "I can't sit out there with all those germs and no immune system."

The physician-in-charge tells us we will have a room soon.

There is no hurry to start me on antibiotics. We wait nearly thirty minutes for a nurse to appear.

When one finally arrives, she is having a bad day and tells us so. To distract her from her bad mood I ask about her unusual necklace.

"It's a Trekkie necklace," she says. "I'm a Trekkie."

She drops the needle she is going to place in my vein on the floor, and I make her day worse by telling her there is no way that needle is going in my arm. Now I am a troublemaker again, and I wish Pierre had one of those wands the doctors use on Star Trek to wave over my body because I know that without my immune system it won't take much for her to kill me if she wants to.

Everyone in Emergency is frazzled. There are not enough doctors and nurses, and too many patients like me who aren't interested in dying tonight.

Pierre leaves the room to find out why a hospital this size can't find a bed for me. As he walks out of the room he overhears the physician-in-charge reaming out the nurses. He purses his lips, points his finger toward their faces, and in a voice that means business says, "We are not going to lose her on my shift." He moves closer to their faces. "Not on *my* shift."

He is talking about me.

Pierre makes phone calls to get prayer support started. While he is gone, I hear him paged. He returns with a strange look on his face.

"Mom called from Miami," he says. "She felt compelled to call today, and Truett told her we were at the hospital but he didn't know which one. She picked this hospital from the list the operator offered and called to say she is already praying."

A nurse enters to announce I have to give up my private room. It is really reserved for women having miscarriages, and one has arrived. They wheel me out into the hallway past a sobbing woman and her bewildered husband.

An orderly pushes me to X-ray and parks me in a waiting area. On a gurney next to me a frail old man vomits into a pink plastic dish shaped like the letter C. I smell the acidic stench and turn away from him, pulling the sheet over my head, in case any of his germs are airborne and coming to attack me without my immune system. Under the thin sheet I hear him vomiting and vomiting until I wonder if he is going to barf up his intestines, and I feel like barfing myself.

After a half-hour in X-ray they finally wheel me in for my turn. Afterwards, an orderly wheels me back to Emergency to a small cubicle with curtains for walls.

On the other side of the curtain a young woman wails because her nose is broken.

"No," she yells, "it hurts."

"You're going to have to let us stop the bleeding," a doctor says in a voice that means she better cooperate or else. From the conversation I overhear I know they are trying to shove something like a tampon up her nose. She lets out a chilling scream.

Pierre goes to the triage counter, and in a voice loud enough for everyone in Emergency to hear he demands the name of the person whose job it is to get us placed in a room.

A young doctor says, "You don't understand the situation, Mr. Asti."

Pierre says loudly, "No, *you* don't understand the situation. I've got a wife who is going to die if she gets exposed to anything down here. We've been here four hours, and nothing has been done to get her into a room."

"I understand," the young doctor says in a patronizing voice.

"No. Don't tell me you understand until you have walked in my shoes." Pierre is firm. "My wife needs a room, and she needs a room now. She must be in a germ-free environment. If you can't get us into a room in the next thirty minutes, we are leaving the hospital, IV and all, for the safety of our home."

A great scurrying begins. Doctors and nurses come into my cubicle about every five minutes to tell us they will have a room for me shortly. Then they find the perfect room, a private room set up for patients who need isolation.

"Where was this room four hours ago?" Pierre asks.

Nobody has an answer.

A nurse wheels me into the hallway just outside a curtained cubicle where a woman loudly describes her abdominal pains and diarrhea to a doctor who is apparently giving her a rectal exam. I try not to picture her big exposed bottom, the doctor with his hand in a latex glove. That is just when a woman wearing a floral jacket and holding a clipboard in her hand stops beside my gurney and cheerfully asks, "Shall we order you some dinner?"

It is nearly ten o'clock when an orderly rolls me into my room. He wheels me on my gurney next to the bed, and I scoot over onto it, shaking. The night nurse brings me a blanket from a warmer to stop my shaking, but I can't stop. The bed is rattling. Pierre doesn't want to leave me, with my shaking and my rattling bed, but Truett is at home and knows nothing except his mom is checking into the hospital.

"Go," I whisper to Pierre. "Truett needs you tonight. I'm just going to sleep."

But I don't sleep. Every time I doze off a nurse comes in to check my vital signs and forgets to turn off the light when she leaves. She is too busy to answer my buzz, so I get out of bed and drag my IV pole across the room to turn off the light. I am finally sleeping soundly for the first time when a crew awakens me at 6:00 A.M. to draw blood.

"Please bring coffee with you tomorrow," I beg, "or I might be the one drawing blood."

Dr. J visits me before seven o'clock. "You steel have de feever," he says. "None of de tests are showing why dis is. Maybe it's de sore throat."

"When can I go home?"

"Twenty-four hours after your feever is gone."

He sits on the side of my bed. He pats my leg. "You luke terrible," he says.

I don't tell him he has never seen me in the morning with my hair sticking out and no makeup. Terrible is normal even under the best conditions.

As he leaves the room I overhear him tell a nurse, "I know dat she will be just fine. I prayed for her in de night."

I shower, still connected to my IV pole, which stands just outside the shower curtain. I blow my hair dry and put on makeup. Then I get back into the bed and realize for the first time that the hospital offers me something unexpectedly that I haven't had for years—time to myself. Time to read. Time to think. I call Pierre with a list of books for him to bring when he comes. A big round clock hangs on the wall below the TV, ticking loudly. Time passes slowly. I have no place to go and nothing to do. I lie back against my pillow. I nap.

My second day in the hospital Dr. J comes late in the morning. I will find out later that he has come in on his day off so I won't have to see a doctor on call I don't know.

"You steel have de fever, but you luke sooo much better dis day," he says. I don't tell him it's because I am wearing makeup.

Flowers arrive from friends and family, but I can't have them in my room because they carry bacteria. Even the flowers with their delicate petals could kill me.

On my bedside table I have a pile of books and a notebook and pen for writing. I take out my Bible study. For the first time I can remember, I have all the time in the world to spend on it because I am in the hospital. I don't have to rush. This is a great gift.

We are studying Genesis, and today I take time to look up at my leisure all the Scriptures listed that describe the Holy Spirit's presence during Creation and other Scriptures that describe different ways the Holy Spirit works. Then a list of verses from John describing Him as a stream of living water for believers, a Counselor who is with us forever, the One who convicts us of our sin. From Romans, I read that He leads the sons of God, He helps us in our weakness, and He intercedes for us. In 2 Corinthians 1:21–22, His Spirit is put in our hearts, as a deposit guaranteeing what is to come.

Then I come across a verse I have read many times in my studies of more than twenty years, yet it seems new to me as I lie in the quiet of my hospital bed with only the sound of the clock ticking loudly across the room. It is 2 Corinthians 3:3. I read it over and over, lean back and let it seep into my brain. "You show that you are a letter from Christ . . . written not with ink but with the Spirit of the living God, not on tablets of stone but on tablets of human hearts."

I am a letter from Christ.

It is a great epiphany for me, as if a moment has arrived that I have been waiting for all my life. Or, rather, it is as if I am entering a moment that has been waiting for me for all eternity. Perhaps unseen angels fill my hospital room, holding their breath, as I recognize that I am a letter from Christ.

After years of thinking that I would write something important for the kingdom of God, my only success is in advertising, and I can't think of anything less important. Now, propped up in this hospital bed, I realize that it doesn't matter at all. I can die without ever writing something weighty. After all, I am a letter from Christ.

He has been busy writing me.

My hair is falling out. When I go to the bathroom I look in the shower stall and see clumps of fine blond hair stuck to the white tile walls. My hair is all over my pillow. If I run my fingers through my hair, it comes out. I crawl to the end of the bed where I can look in the mirror over my sink. I still look normal, but this will not last.

After dinner, Pierre brings Truett to visit so that he can see that I am OK. Fifteen and tall, he stands shyly across the room wearing his baggy shorts and his baseball cap backwards. He has never seen his mother in a hospital with tubes coming out of her arms.

"Look at this." I show him how I can adjust the bed.

He comes closer to look. I move over and pat the bed. He lies down beside me. I show him the TV buttons on the bedrail. He smiles, his eyes full of mischief. He pushes buttons to raise our feet, then our heads, nearly folding us in half.

"You've got it made, Mom." He flips on the TV and uses his thumb to point to a plastic bedpan across the room. "See that over there. You can watch anything you want, and you don't even have to get up to go to the bathroom if you don't want to."

When I wake up on the third day in the hospital, a lot more of my hair is gone but so is my fever. This means I can go home tomorrow, in time for Labor Day weekend. Dr. J visits me late in the afternoon and is elated to see my vital signs.

"You luke like Meese Amereeka dis day," he says.

He sits on the side of my bed.

I ask, "Can I have my flowers now?"

He pushes the button to ring the nurses' station. When they answer, he says in his highest falsetto voice, "Please bring me de flowers. Dr. J sayz I can have dem now." The nurses laugh.

A nurse enters with vases of flowers.

"Oooh, dey are sooo preety," Dr. J says, still in falsetto.

It is Friday before Labor Day weekend. I can go home today. Pierre arrives and finds me dressed, packed, and waiting. He loads the flowers onto a rolling cart. I ride in a wheelchair down to the hospital entrance.

On the way home I ask Pierre if we have any invitations for the weekend.

"No," he says. "Everyone knows you have been in the hospital."

I am weak, but I am still disappointed that we have no invitations to do anything fun for the weekend.

On Saturday, Pierre drives me by the old houses I love in a nearby community, but they don't interest me.

"You're not yourself today," Pierre says.

"I'm already sick of being nothing but a cancer patient, and I'm just at the beginning."

"You're doing great. I'm proud of you."

"It's Labor Day weekend, and we should be having fun with friends."

"They are just giving you time to get strong."

"I don't want time. I want to do normal things, talk about normal things."

"What is that supposed to mean?"

"I'm sick of talking about cancer. Nobody talks to me about anything else. That's what my life has become—cancer. I am nothing but a cancer patient."

"You're still Judy."

"That's the point. I feel like I'm just that poor woman with breast cancer now."

X   X   X

Monday night Pierre shaves off what little is left of my hair. Then we sit in the warm swirling water of the spa to relax. I wear a baseball cap because my head is cold. I cry in the dark. Labor Day weekend ends with me laboring with God about what has become of my life. This doesn't feel anything like heaven.

JOURNEY SURVIVAL GUIDE

At times on the cancer journey our circumstances shout so loudly that it is difficult to hear the still small voice of our Lord. But that doesn't mean He isn't speaking. If we keep standing firmly in faith through the storm we will hear Him once again.

> *The LORD said [to Elijah], "Go out and stand on the mountain in the presence of the LORD, for the LORD is about to pass by."*
> *Then a great and powerful wind tore the mountains apart and shattered the rocks before the LORD, but the LORD was not in the wind. After the wind there was an earthquake, but the LORD was not in the earthquake. After the earthquake came a fire, but the*

*LORD was not in the fire. And after
the fire came a gentle whisper.*
1 Kings 19:11–12

Four

ALL IS VANITY

Charm is deceptive, and beauty is fleeting;
but a woman who fears the LORD is to be praised.
—◦ PROVERBS 31:30 ◦—

When the author of Ecclesiastes, thought to be the wise King Solomon himself, wrote about the vanity of everything under the sun or, in other words, everything without God, it is interesting that he never once mentioned the vanity of our outward physical appearance. He discussed our striving for pleasure and possessions, our work and wealth, and even the vanity of life itself without God. However, he omitted our efforts to improve our looks. Could it be that he could not envision our world as it is today with the billions of dollars we spend each year to make ourselves appear more beautiful to other people? Or was it just such a given that we humans are like this, and were even in his day, that it wasn't even worth mentioning? We live in a world that bows down to the god of beauty.

X   X   X

A true "bad hair day" is when you wake up in the morning, look in the mirror, and remember that you have no hair at all.

I stare at myself in the bathroom mirror. The overhead fixture beams down its light on my head that is so completely bald it shines. I am no longer a woman. I am a melon with a face.

There are plenty of women who look beautiful with no hair, like the movie stars who shave their heads for special films. I am not one of them.

I am a woman who is not naturally beautiful, living in a world where beauty is a god, and because of it I grew up—as did many of the women I know—insecure about my looks.

I am a vain woman.

I continue working throughout my cancer treatments; and my work, in advertising, is all about image. I have no intention of going to work bald. I want a great wig.

I have not left this to chance, being vain, and neither should you. Some chemotherapies almost always cause hair loss. Ask your doctor. There are plenty of women who wear hats and scarves that are a dead give-away that they are cancer patients, and they are fine with it, and still others who wear their baldness like a badge. I say more power to them. However, if you want a wig, go shopping *before* your hair falls out, to ease the trauma.

I go to many stores and try on inexpensive wigs. They resemble something like Halloween wigs on my small head. Then I find a wig salon that specializes in exact hair duplication. Here, a soft-spoken man takes pictures of my hair from all angles and holds swatches of hair up to my head to match the color. These wigs are expensive, at a thousand dollars, but I will wear mine every day for nearly a year. I consider it money well spent.

My mother and my brother chip in on the purchase, and I place the order so that after I go home from the hospital and my hair is gone, my wig is waiting for me on the Tuesday after Labor Day. I drive to the salon early in the morning wearing a baseball cap.

A woman leads me to a private room and seats me in a swivel chair before a regular beauty shop station. She explains that it will be a long morning, but if I will just be patient, the results will be worth the wait. She drapes a pink plastic cape over my shoulders and ties it around my neck. She removes my baseball cap and sets it on the counter in front of me. Then she rubs my bald head with her bare hands. It is a delicious feeling, and the tenderness of the moment takes me by surprise.

For the next two hours she transforms the wig to look like my own hair. First, she fits the inner elastic cap to my head, tucking and sewing in stages to get an exact fit so that the wind won't blow my hair off. Then she cuts and thins the wig hair to match the hair in the pictures previously taken. I watch in the mirror as she gradually reduces an enormous mane of hair and I begin to look like myself again. Then she whips the wig off my head.

"Now the finishing touches," she says.

"What finishing touches?"

"All highlighted blondes have roots," she says. "Your wig is too bright without them, and besides you need them to add depth. Watch on television—even the movie stars have roots."

I sit in the swivel chair and flip through a magazine, thinking of all the money I have spent in the past ten years to avoid dark roots. However, when she returns and puts the wig on my head I stare in the mirror. The wig looks exactly like my real hair. Only better, because it's the best head of hair I ever had.

At work nobody notices my hair. When the company chairman walks into my office, I am sitting at the computer with my back to him. He alone knows where I spent the morning. I turn around slowly, and I can tell by the look on his face that he is not at all positive I have told him the truth.

By afternoon I have a splitting headache from the elastic squeezing my head and I want to rip the wig off, but I can't. I am bald.

When I arrive home from work, Truett is there. It takes him three looks before he remembers I was bald when he left for school in the morning.

"That's awesome, Mom," he says. "I couldn't even tell."

My wig looks real. I go up to my room, carefully take it off and place it on the Styrofoam headform on my dressing table. I rub my sore head and go downstairs where Pierre is preparing dinner. My family will have to get used to a bald mom.

To experience what it is like to wear a wig all day, take a pair of panty hose, preferably sized for a small child so that the elastic is very tight, and wear the panty hose on your head for twelve hours.

⚕   ⚕   ⚕

There are three more treatments of Adriamycin and Cytoxan, twenty-one days apart. Now, the dose is reduced, and I learn to avoid germs in order to stay out of the hospital. At work I post a sign outside my office forbidding anyone with symptoms of any disease known to man from entering. I keep hand sanitizers on my desk, in my purse, and in my car. In public restrooms I don't touch anything without paper towels. In the middle of the chemo cycle, when my blood count is at its lowest, I don't go anywhere unnecessarily.

What in normal circumstances might be considered paranoia is just plain smart for a chemotherapy patient. It is essential to avoid germs when your white blood count is low. Whenever possible stay away from anyone you know is ill, strangers, and crowds. Use hand sanitizers frequently. Do not eat salads or other uncooked foods unless you know they have been thoroughly washed.

The nausea returns with each treatment. The chemotherapy damages the lining of my digestive tract, so painful sores appear in my mouth and my stomach can't handle spicy food.

The chemotherapy brings on instant menopause. Hot flashes

flare up at work. Throughout the day I turn on my desk fan and remove my jacket with the onset of each hot flash. Then when it's over I put my jacket back on and turn off the fan. On, off; on, off. All day. At home I put away my silky pajamas and borrow my son's cotton T-shirt and boxer shorts to tolerate the night sweats that wake me drenched and fitful.

It seems as if every week catalogs arrive at my home from Victoria's Secret. I know I should just toss them in the trash, but instead I torture myself by opening them. There, on the glossy pages, women show off their amazing bodies and especially beautiful breasts. I am reminded on a regular basis that soon one of my own will be removed. A date in November has been set for my mastectomy.

My office phone rings. The mother of my son's friend asks for my help with a project.

"I have breast cancer," I tell her. "I'm in the middle of chemotherapy and trying to work. That's all I can handle."

"BREAST CANCER," she shouts. "Oh, I didn't know. Is it in one or two?"

I am silent at this intrusive question—in one or two? I let it hang in the air for seconds. Then I say simply, "I'm sorry, I can't help you."

In one or two?

I know this woman. She is kindhearted and she meant no harm in asking this. She was simply insensitive, because even the best of us are not well equipped to handle conversation regarding cancer. And I am not equipped to handle this insensitivity, having never had breast cancer before. I hang up the phone, and the heat of anger rises out of my own pain at knowing that I am about to lose a breast and that I live in a world that simply adores breasts.

Why would anyone who is not one of my closest confidants ask that question—in one or two? Does she want to imagine what I will look like when the doctors get through with me?

I have never been quick on my feet. Now, sitting at my desk with the phone receiver back on its cradle, I think of my response to such a question. "Let's talk about *your* breasts first. Then we'll talk about mine."

My reaction is as thoughtless as her question, but I don't realize it yet. I am in pain. I have heard the gamut of success and horror stories regarding reconstruction. Pierre repeatedly reassures me that it doesn't matter to him if I even have reconstruction, he just wants me. I know he means it. But I can't help wondering if he also imagines what I will look like when the doctors get through with me and whether he will ever again be able to look at me naked without turning his head away.

I can sleep an extra thirty minutes in the mornings now because I don't have to wash and blow-dry my hair or shave my hairless legs. I am getting dressed for work. For some reason, I still have eyebrows and eyelashes. When I am put together I still look pretty normal. Extra blush camouflages the chemotherapy pallor. I apply mascara. Then the last thing I do before I walk out the door is put on my wig. Although it is rather permanently styled, it has to be brushed each day to look fresh. I am in a hurry, and I brush fast. My brush catches the inner cap of the wig, lifts it from my head and hurls it across the bedroom like a flying squirrel. I gasp, shocked by the instant sight of myself bald again. Then I laugh until tears roll down my cheeks.

Pierre pokes his head out of the bathroom where he is shaving. "What's so funny?" he asks.

"I guess this is where we get the expression 'She flipped her wig!'"

I receive a letter from Dan Yeary, my first pastor, who baptized me more than twenty-five years ago. In it he tells me, "Nothing on earth will mar your beauty, because it comes from an enormous, endless resource that God has provided and will continue to provide."

Standing in my kitchen with the letter in my hands, I begin to weep. I have remained so focused on my outer appearance, an appearance that is increasingly becoming unrecognizable when the wig and the makeup come off, that I am forgetting to look for what God is doing on the inside. This pastor who pointed me to God in the first place now points me back to Him as I face the biggest battle of my life.

It is time to begin looking to see what God is doing on the inside.

In the days that follow it occurs to me that I am far stronger than I ever imagined. In the beginning I was ready to lie down and die of cancer. Now I find myself fully engaged in the battle, not as a helpless victim but as an aggressive opponent, reading everything I can get my hands on about breast cancer. I now think of food as fuel. I switch from my dozen cups of coffee a day to green tea. I drink soy milk. I take dozens of vitamins a week. I find a natural deodorant. I focus on lowering my stress level, leaving the family room when a television show becomes violent or stressful, which means I hardly ever watch television at all. Pierre and the answering machine screen my telephone calls so that I only talk to positive people. I am a woman with a mission.

I am scraping paint off the ceiling in the master bath shower, a place nobody sees except Pierre and me, when I realize that God is doing something else as well.

The rooms that people see on the main floor of our home look inviting because we spent the past two years refurbishing them. Yet here in the shower, I work in a private place, hidden from guests. Old peeling paint hangs in tiny bits over the entire surface. I scrape until my arms ache and then use an electric sander on the remaining loose bits. The vibration of the sander blows the light bulb, but I have plenty of natural light from the window. I am shaking the can of paint when Pierre replaces the light bulb for me. With that bright supernatural light shining I can see tiny bits of old peeling paint still clinging to the ceiling.

I am like my house. God knows the hidden places where only His supernatural light can get to the bottom of things. I am a vain woman, concerned about the outside, always worrying about what other people think. Indeed, I am in great need of a makeover, but not the kind you receive at a beauty salon. God has work to do on the inside, in the hidden places.

One night I need a prescription from the pharmacy, and no one else is home. After a long day at work I feel so sick I can't bear the thought of putting my wig back on. Reluctantly, I put a baseball cap on my bald head and drive to the drugstore, praying all the way there that no one will be in the store. There is a line at the pharmacy in the back of the drugstore at least ten people long. I have to stand in it. I nervously look around to see if there is anyone I know.

And then something strange happens. I realize that nobody is paying any attention to my baldness even though it is evident despite the baseball cap. People are entirely absorbed with their own needs. They chat in line about the inconvenience of waiting. They talk to me without staring. They pick up their prescriptions and leave the store. Life goes on as always. The world does not stop turning because I am not put together.

$$\text{ᛒ} \qquad \text{ᛒ} \qquad \text{ᛒ}$$

My pastor is preaching out of Ecclesiastes when a line in the text catches my attention. "He has made everything beautiful in its time. He has also set eternity in the hearts of men; yet they cannot fathom what God has done from beginning to end" (3:11).

He has made *everything* beautiful in its time. That includes me. I know that I am created in His image, but surely God is not a tall, bald woman with a body that is getting too thin from cancer. Yet there is something about me that is like Him. Could it be the eternity He has set in my heart?

Perhaps the apostle Paul had a clue of what it means to be made in God's image when he wrote: "God has chosen to make known among the Gentiles the glorious riches of this mystery, which is Christ in you, the hope of glory" (Colossians 1:27). And later in the same book: "In Christ all the fullness of the Deity lives in bodily form, and you have been given fullness in Christ, who is the head over every power and authority (2:9–10).

Christ in me, the hope of glory. In Him all the fullness of God dwells—and I have been given that fullness, too. It is a profound mystery, and yet Paul gives us a glimpse of the splendor that is ours if we have Christ in us. The outer body is simply a shell that will carry me through this life, but the inner me will go on to glory.

Cancer causes the outer me to become unrecognizable when I am at home. Without my wig or makeup I have a gray cast to my skin, I am painfully thin, and of course I am completely bald. Focusing on my outward appearance becomes unbearable, and so it is actually cancer that enables me to get beyond it to focus on what's inside me, which is Christ.

"Man looks at the outward appearance, but the LORD looks at the heart" (1 Samuel 16:7). Does He see Himself there? Can I?

JOURNEY SURVIVAL GUIDE

The journey is tough on the body. There is a lot you can do to maintain a pretty normal appearance if you want to, but try not to dwell on it. Despite what Hollywood tells us, the outer body is simply a vessel that carries us through this life. Keep your eyes off the mirror and on the Lord. It is the inner life that really matters. Moreover, if Christ dwells there, you will go on to heaven. Paul said it this way:

> *When Christ, who is your life,*
> *appears, then you also will appear*
> *with him in glory.*
>   Colossians 3:4

Five

A HEAVENLY FORETASTE

Now we see but a poor reflection as in a mirror;
then we shall see face to face. Now I know in part;
then I shall know fully, even as I am fully known.
And now these three remain; faith, hope and love.
But the greatest of these is love.

—◦ 1 CORINTHIANS 13:12–13 ◦—

E*verything is against me!"* the Jewish patriarch Jacob says in Genesis 42. Jacob believes his beloved son Joseph has been dead for years, although he is actually in Egypt running the show, the second most powerful man in the nation. A famine strikes, and Jacob sends his remaining sons, except for Benjamin, the youngest, from Canaan to Egypt to buy grain.

When they arrive in Egypt, they don't recognize that it is their very brother Joseph, whom they had sold into slavery years before, who is in charge of the grain distribution. Longing to see his brother Benjamin, Joseph does not reveal his identity and demands that one of the brothers remain in Egypt while the rest return to Canaan and bring Benjamin back. Joseph gives his men orders to fill his brothers' sacks with grain and to hide in the sacks the silver they brought for the purchase.

Simeon remains while the others return home to break the news to Jacob that they must take Benjamin. They empty the sacks and discover the silver. Terrified, Jacob says to his sons, "You have deprived me of my children. Joseph is no more and Simeon is no more, and now you want to take Benjamin. Everything is against me!" (Genesis 42:36).

"Everything is against me!" That statement is laughable from our vantage point some thirty-five hundred years later as we watch the story unfold. It is easy for us to see that God has been working on Jacob's behalf all along. Jacob is blessed beyond imagination. God's brilliant plan is both intricate and global in nature, not only to save Jacob's entire family but also to fulfill the promise He made to Abraham that from his seed would come the Messiah.

Still, in all fairness to Jacob, he can't see what we see. He can only see his current circumstances, so he wallows in fear and self-pity.

It is easy on the cancer journey to feel that "everything is against me." For I am caught up in the daily realities of treatments, appointments with doctors, time missed at work, having my sore fingers poked for more blood, looking ugly, and often feeling so sick that death appears to be an attractive alternative. Like Jacob, I can't see my situation from God's point of view. I can see only my own circumstances, and on many days they overwhelm me.

In my life, however, an unseen reality is also unfolding. In my case, God's plan for my cancer journey began long before my diagnosis, at least a full year before, when He led our family to change churches.

At that time we were members of a megachurch but not very plugged in. One day, folding clothes in my bedroom, I am aware that if we have a major family crisis we will have no one to minister to us. We live hundreds of miles from our families in a city where we have not yet made any close friends. Our aloof and scholarly pastor rarely recognizes us. We are disconnected from the body of Christ.

That night Pierre and I discuss the need to change churches, and then the next Sunday an odd thing happens. We are all sick except for Pierre, and he is on his way to church, driving the usual route, when he has an overwhelming urge to turn left where he would ordinarily turn right. Perhaps King Solomon had a similar experience, for he writes, "In his heart a man plans his course, but the LORD determines his steps" (Proverbs 16:9). Pierre turns left and ends up attending Bloomfield Hills Baptist Church, a small church near our home.

The following Sunday, and for several Sundays afterwards, we return to our old church. Then one Sunday, another odd thing happens. We are sitting in worship surrounded by a sea of strangers. The boys immediately go to sleep when the sermon begins, and I become an idiot.

For some reason, I simply cannot understand a word the pastor says. I try taking notes to stay with him, but I cannot make sense out of anything. It is as if God has quite literally stopped up my ears. I lean over to Pierre and whisper, "Who is he preaching to?"

Pierre shrugs.

In the car on the ride home we bring up the idea of looking for a new church. Pierre says, "Lance, we'll wait until you leave for college."

Lance immediately answers, "Why wait?"

Why wait, indeed? The very next Sunday we visit Bloomfield Hills Baptist Church as a family. The service and singing are joyful, Pastor Cliff Powell is biblical and straightforward, and afterwards teens literally run across the sanctuary to welcome our sons.

We immediately sense we have arrived at our church home, and we are still there today. The reason this is part of my cancer story is because of the profound role this small church plays in my healing process.

We have been members only a year when my diagnosis comes and we are not intimately known by many. It makes no difference at all. From the moment my cancer is announced in the Wednesday night prayer meeting the wheels that set ministry in motion begin turning.

My friend Sherrie Cooke takes charge of meals. She buys a special calendar just for my needs and enlists an army of people to cook. With every chemotherapy treatment, church members deliver dinner to our family for as many days as we need.

Now I am a working mother, and dinner at our house often consists of some ready-made concoction that is microwaved beyond recognition. In stark contrast, the meals brought by church members are feasts. Church members arrive at the door smiling, their arms laden with healthy meals made from scratch, huge pots of soups and stews, steaming casseroles, fresh fruit cut up in bowls, crisp salads, warm bread, and homemade desserts. Often they even bring flowers for the table, and always they bring enough food to last for days.

They are serving up their love for Christ and, because of Him, for us, in covered dishes. They stay around just long enough to know that our needs are met; then they leave us with a meal fit for the King. When our family sits at the table to eat, the love and generosity of our church family overwhelms us. We bow our heads in heartfelt thanks. "We continually remember before our God and Father your work produced by faith, your labor prompted by love, and your endurance inspired by hope in our Lord Jesus Christ" (1 Thessalonians 1:3).

The church feeds us in other ways as well. Cards pour in from people I know and don't know, and they will continue to arrive for a full year, long after my last treatment has ended. They share with me their special Bible verses, their own experiences with God in hard times. They tell me they are praying. And they don't just tell me they are praying, they pray, not just privately, but publicly, tenderly, intimately, and in detail during our Wednesday night prayer meetings and on Sunday mornings. I attend many times even when I am very sick, because hearing their prayers lifts my spirit and gives me hope.

We have belonged to churches that were bigger, more beautiful, more musically talented, and more socially minded. But never more loving. They become a kind of extended family to us who live so far away from our blood families.

Surely this is something of what Jesus means when He says, "No one who has left home or brothers or sisters or mother or father or children or fields for me and the gospel will fail to receive a hundred times as much in this present age" (Mark 10:29–30).

During this same time, I am also a small group discussion leader for Bible Study Fellowship (BSF), an interdenominational Bible study with nearly a thousand classes in twenty-eight countries. Although I love serving in this ministry, staying on during my illness is selfish on my part because I don't want to give up the Saturday morning leaders' meetings.

We meet at 6:55 A.M. Saturdays are my only days to sleep in. However, during the school year when BSF is in session, I get up at 5:30 A.M. to get to the meetings on time. In Michigan, this often means leaving in total darkness with below zero temperatures and icy roads. Yet, as I drive into the parking lot of the church where we meet, my car just beginning to thaw from the freezing drive, I look up at the second story windows, where bright light streams out into the black morning, and warmth rises up within me.

Here, I am surrounded by women who put my spiritual life to shame. When I walk up the stairs to that second floor room, these devoted women also greet me with hugs. But it is not the hugs that get me out of bed before dawn. It is the prayer.

In that upstairs room some thirty of us sit on blue folding chairs placed in a tight circle. Our leader reads the prayer requests and we slip out of our chairs, drop to our knees, and pray aloud. Every week they shower me with prayer, and I feel the power of it washing over me, lifting me to a new level of hopefulness.

Cancer patients are generally referred to cancer support groups where they can share their stories, talk openly about their fears, and receive help from others on the same journey. In the best of these groups there is a positive mood, an attitude of overcoming that is a vital lifeline. However, I choose not to join such a group because I don't want to spend my limited time talking about cancer. Instead, this group of godly women and the faithful members of my church become my support group. I spend every Saturday and Sunday morning and every Sunday, Monday, and Wednesday night talking instead about the awesome power of the Lord. It has a profound effect on my thought process about my future, both in this life and the next.

Word of my cancer and the seriousness of the diagnosis spreads among my network of friends and family throughout the country. I receive cards, letters, calls, books, flowers and e-mails on a daily basis. "Pray for each other so that you may be healed" (James 5:16). All over the country, churches add my name to their prayer lists. Literally thousands of people are praying for me now. Our entire family feels buoyed up by this outpouring of love and massive petitioning to God for victory.

As the date for my surgery approaches, I have no plastic surgeon for the reconstruction. I want to use Dr. Sherbert, but he has gone out on his own into a solitary practice and is not yet approved by my insurance.

I am referred to a plastic surgeon who has an office an hour from my home. When I arrive, I am led to a private examination room and told to undress and put on a paper vest before I meet the doctor. He walks into the room wearing hospital scrubs and shiny black formal shoes that look out of place. He tells me his name. Then he asks, "What is your bra size?"

I am surprised by the brusqueness of this question, and I mumble my size. Without any conversation to put me at ease he walks over to me, opens my vest and palpitates my breasts as if they were a couple of peaches in a grocery store bin.

"You'll always be lopsided," he says bluntly. Then he makes me look at pictures of women he has reconstructed that do, indeed, look lopsided.

I pay my ten dollar co-pay and cry during the hour-long drive home.

Now I want Dr. Sherbert to be my plastic surgeon even more. He has been waiting months for the certification from my insurance company, but as my surgery date approaches it doesn't look promising.

I turn in a prayer request at BSF that Dr. Sherbert's paperwork will come through in time, and the leaders drop to their knees to pray.

I receive a call exactly one week before my surgery that Dr. Sherbert has not only been approved by my insurance company but that he has an opening on the day of my scheduled surgery. Everything is not against me. God is for me.

Cancer is an emotional roller-coaster ride. The week prior to surgery I can't stop crying. I am having my breast removed on the Thursday before Thanksgiving. I can't imagine feeling thankful at all.

On Saturday I go to the leaders meeting of BSF, and they pray for me. On Sunday morning many people at church come up to us and hug us and tell us they are praying for us. On Monday night I go to the BSF general meeting, and the leaders pray for me again. With each passing day my confidence increases. We are warriors being equipped with everything we need. They are preparing us for battle, and the battle belongs to the Lord.

It is the Wednesday night before my surgery. I am lying in bed with Pierre, feeling surprisingly at ease. I turn to him in the dark and whisper, "You know, it's weird, I'm bald, I'm having a mastectomy tomorrow, and after all this I still might die of cancer. But I am at perfect peace."

Pierre holds me close and is silent for a few seconds. Then he whispers back, "Me too."

It is another wave that is washing over us as we lie embracing each other in the dark, but this time it is what the apostle Paul calls the peace that transcends understanding. We have never recognized it so clearly before.

The peace lingers. With a modified radical mastectomy scheduled for the next morning, we sleep the blissful, sound sleep of babies. It is as if we are lifted up in a heavenly capsule of protection that no power on this earth can penetrate.

On the morning of my surgery we sing songs of praise to God in the shower. We drive to the hospital relaxed, like infants held in the strong arms of a loving father.

We arrive at the hospital at 6:00 A.M., fill out paperwork, and are quickly taken to a holding area where a nurse escorts us to a private curtained cubicle and hands me a hospital gown. I undress, slip into the gown, and hop up on the gurney. Pierre is tucking the covers around me when our pastor, Cliff Powell, arrives. Slightly younger than we, he is a rather small man, with an enormous pastor's heart. His eyes are moist. He holds a small Bible with a battered leather cover the color of a well-worn saddle. And as he opens it to read a passage, we all mount up together to ride out the tough terrain that lies ahead. He reads, "I will lie down and sleep in peace, for you alone, O LORD, make me dwell in safety" (Psalm 4:8).

JOURNEY SURVIVAL GUIDE

Sometimes, in a crisis such as cancer, Christians battling bitterness turn away from God and His people. Yet this is just when we most need to turn to the Lord and His church. It is vital to be connected to the body of Christ. It is often through our church, Bible study, or small group that God ministers to us. When people offer help, accept it. Be specific, since most people don't really know what is most helpful. Tell them you need dinner delivered the night of chemo, or a ride to a treatment. I longed for fresh fruit but was too tired to peel and cut. I asked my friends to help, and they delivered big bowls of delicious mixed fruit.

Do not be anxious about anything, but in everything, by prayer and petition, with thanksgiving, present your requests to God. And the peace of God, which transcends all understanding, will guard your hearts and your minds in Christ Jesus.
Philippians 4:6–7

Six

MOTHER LOVE

As a mother comforts her child,
so will I comfort you.
—✿ ISAIAH 66:13 ✿—

I t is time for surgery. I ride on my gurney to a ward where about ten patients are being prepared for surgeries of all kinds. Pierre is allowed to go with me this far. Patients on gurneys line both sides of the room facing each other. Machines beep and whir. Nurses and technicians hurry about their business, wearing colorful hospital scrubs—purple, blue, green, floral—attending their patients. White curtains are half-drawn between patients so I can't see who is on either side of me.

Dr. Benitez, who will perform the mastectomy, and Dr. Sherbert, who will begin the reconstruction, arrive within minutes and pull the curtains all the way around my gurney to form a small, private cubicle. Dr. Sherbert asks me to stand beside the gurney and lower my hospital gown to my waist.

It is the last time in my life I will ever look down and see my breasts as they are. My eyes well up with tears so I can barely see them.

The two doctors discuss the plan of action and agree on the location and size of the incision. Dr. Sherbert draws a horizontal line on my breast with a black marker where the incision will be that is longer than I had hoped, and vertical lines to give himself perspective once the breast tissue has been removed.

I pull my gown on and get back up on the gurney. The doctors leave to prepare for surgery. A nurse opens the curtains and inserts a needle into a vein in my wrist. I am drowsy within minutes. The nurse removes my baseball cap and hands it to Pierre. She gives me a thin paper cap with elastic all the way around to wear although I have no hair to cover.

Pierre kisses me good-bye on the mouth. "I love you," he says.

"I love you, too," I mumble sleepily.

I am wheeled out of my space, and I float down the hall in a fog. The last thing I remember is passing Dr. Sherbert, who is standing in the hallway, and in my drug-induced stupor I lift my hand to him and say, "There's no place like home . . ."

If I awakened in recovery, I don't remember it. I remember only waking up in a semi-private room with Pierre sitting in a chair at the end of the bed, looking drawn. He comes to stand beside me and takes my hand.

"Everything went great," he says. "It took longer than expected because Dr. Benitez was so careful. You have so little body fat around your lymph nodes she had to go slowly to avoid nerve damage. Dr. Sherbert says everything was set up perfectly for him and the tissue expander is all inserted."

Under the covers I move my hand to my breast. There is a bandaged breast mound where a rubbery saline-filled implant builds my chest so that I am not flat-chested on the surgery side. This tissue expander minimizes the immediate disfiguration from the mastectomy. It is temporary and will remain in my body until

I have completed radiation treatments. Before radiation begins, Dr. Sherbert will add saline every two weeks to a port attached to the expander, increasing it to larger than my other breast to maximize the amount of skin available for the final reconstruction. Afterwards a permanent implant will be inserted.

This is one time in my life when it is detrimental to be thin. I was not a candidate for the Transverse Rectus Abdominis Muscle (TRAM) Flap procedure where they tunnel skin, fat, blood vessels, and muscles from the abdomen, under the rib cage and to the chest, leaving the blood supply intact. This creates a soft, fatty breast and gives the added bonus of a free tummy tuck. I have too little abdominal fat to utilize for this reconstruction.

As I feel the new breast mound I am surprised to discover that I have two plastic tubes sticking out of my breast. I follow them with my hand. They lead to two plastic vials. I push back the covers and lift my hospital gown. The vials are full of blood. I dislike the sight of blood, especially my own, and I stare in horror at these tubes with blood moving slowly through them into these blood-filled vials.

I am too exhausted to deal with it. I pull the covers up and lie back. My paper hat is gone. My bald head is cold.

I ask, "Where's my baseball cap?"

"Trevor has it," Pierre says.

"Trevor's here?"

"He borrowed a car to drive home from State to be with us for the surgery. Let me go out and tell everybody you're awake."

Everybody turns out to be Pierre, Trevor, Mom, and Jean MacKay, a close friend who drove an hour to sit with Pierre throughout the morning and into the afternoon. She was there as the doctors gave their reports following the surgery. When Pierre calls them, they crowd into my side of the small room.

Jean is sixty-something, a tiny blond dynamo that is more family to me than friend. She was our real estate agent when we moved to Michigan, and we hit it off immediately. With two grown sons of her own, she is one of my favorite resources for advice.

"Hey, kiddo," she says, "I don't know where you found those doctors, but if I ever have what you got, I want *them*."

I know that I had not "found" the doctors. I was providentially led to them.

There aren't enough chairs for everybody to sit. Pierre insists that Mom sit down.

Jean and Trevor stand on either side of my bed. Trevor kisses me on my bald head and puts my baseball cap on it. I don't care who sees me bald now. I look at them all through the haze that remains from the anesthesia. I see the stress on their faces as I try to emerge from the fog. My mouth is dry. I motion, and Jean hands me a Styrofoam cup of ice water. I take a sip, and she puts it back on my nightstand.

I gradually become more alert, and we talk in low voices trying not to disturb my roommate, whom we have not seen on the other side of the curtain that divides our room. As I become more animated, relief is evident on Trevor and Jean's faces. Finally, they kiss me good-bye and squeeze my toes through the covers on the way out of the room, heading back to all they have put on hold.

For the duration of the afternoon, Pierre and Mom sit in vinyl-covered chairs watching me doze.

The room grows darker as the afternoon passes. I look at Mom, seventy-five years old, still attractive, but now she looks especially weary.

"Go home and have dinner," I beg them. "Truett's going to be coming home from school to an empty house."

"I'll stay," Mom says. "Pierre, you go home."

"No," I insist. "I'll be fine. I'm just going to sleep. Go eat. I need you to be strong when I get home."

They agree to go home to Truett.

They leave as my dinner arrives, and I immediately regret sending them away. I don't really want to be alone. However, I won't allow myself the luxury of feeling sorry for myself. Not yet, anyway. I am not certain why I feel I have to be strong, but I will pay a high price for it later.

It is unnecessary to make everyone around you miserable, but important not to completely repress your feelings. Emotional healing actually comes faster if you allow yourself time to grieve. Just don't stay there.

I push the button to raise the head of my bed and lift the chrome covers off my dinner. A television hangs from the ceiling not far from the foot of my bed. I turn on the TV to watch the evening news, but it doesn't interest me. I snap it off.

When I finish eating, a nurse comes in to show me how to "milk" the tubes jutting from my breast using my thumb and fingers to push the blood into the vials.

She empties the blood-filled vials into a measuring beaker and records the amount and color of the blood in a little booklet. I watch her do it for me; then, after she leaves, I reach over to my bedside table for a pink plastic dish shaped like the letter C and vomit up my dinner.

The evening drags on. Nausea and loneliness are my only visitors. Everyone is giving me "time" after this emotional surgery. I wish someone, anyone, would barge into my room for conversation. I call my sister in Atlanta, but I get her answering machine. I turn the television on and off several times. I try to read. Nothing interests me.

Finally, it is respectably late enough to go to bed for the night. My nurse gives me a pill to help me sleep, but it isn't strong enough. I can't get comfortable. I sleep lightly and wake throughout the night. Finally, as dawn is nearing, I drift off into a deep sleep. That's when the fire alarm goes off at the hospital. The screeching siren lurches me awake. I lie still, wondering what we patients are supposed to do. I imagine all the patients shuffling out of their rooms pushing their IV poles with one hand, holding their gowns together in the back with the other. I glance at the clock. It is 5:00 A.M. I sniff the air for smoke, detect none, and decide to take my chances, pulling the covers over my shoulders. I hear nurses scurrying. I push my button to ring the nurses' station, but they don't answer.

It turns out there is no fire, just a little fire drill that cost all the patients, on my hall at least, whatever sleep it is possible to get in a hospital. Just as I go back to sleep, breakfast arrives.

It isn't long before a doctor I don't know comes in and asks to look at my breast.

I resist, asking, "Who sent you?" I am tired of showing my breasts to strangers, and I'm not going to further anyone's education with this one.

He apologizes and tells me Dr. Benitez can't get in this morning and has asked him to sign off on the release papers. I untie my gown and let him see the bandaged mound.

"Everything looks good. You can go home as soon as you are ready," he says.

I translate that to mean the hospital needs my bed. One night of care is all you're entitled to for a modified radical mastectomy these days. I call Pierre to come and get me, and since I am still wobbly and my arm on the surgery side is sore and rather useless from having lymph nodes removed from my armpit, an impatient nurse helps me get dressed.

Pierre finds me sitting on the bed with my suitcase packed.

At home it is my mother who will be my caretaker for the next week and a half. There is a mother-daughter "thing," and my mother and I have it. She has always been very close to my brother and my sister but was never particularly close to me. Nevertheless, it is into the care of my mother that I arrive home from the hospital wearing my shirttail out to hide the blood-filled vials connected to the tubes hanging out of my temporarily reconstructed breast. Pierre helps me upstairs, settles me in our bed, and goes to the office to try to put in a few hours of work.

Mom comes in and out of my bedroom periodically to see if I need anything. There is surprisingly little physical pain associated with the surgery. I lie propped up on pillows and stare out the window at my backyard two stories down, grateful, even though it is caused by this particular surgery, for the time off from work.

As I look out the window I can see squirrels scampering along the top of the wooden fence and into the trees. Canada geese pass over in the sky on their way south. It feels strange that life goes on just as it always has when it has come to such a standstill for me. Our good friends are building their dream homes and taking dream vacations. For the most part, the people I know are still going about their own ordinary business, their cycle of life as it has always been. My business has become the all-consuming battle against this life-threatening disease. For some reason, it is a surprise that all of life is not all consumed with my disease, too.

Late in the afternoon Mom comes in, and I move my legs over so she can sit at the foot of my bed. She stares out the window for a few minutes, looking weary. Her gray hair is slightly disheveled. I think of the Lord's command: "Honor your father and your mother, so that you may live long in the land the LORD your God is giving you" (Exodus 20:12).

She examines her hands in her lap and then says, "I wish I could take your place."

"What do you mean?"

"I wish I could have the cancer and you could be well. I've lived a good life. You kids are grown and happy. I've known my grandchildren. Dad is gone. If I could take this cancer from you and have it myself, I would do it. I just want you to know that."

I stare at Mom in disbelief. She has never said anything like this to me before, and I can tell by the way her face contorts, her eyes brimming with tears when she looks at me, that she means it.

I reach out and hold her hand in silence. I am surprised by the softness of Mom's hands.

It is Saturday morning. Pierre is leaving for the office to try to reduce the mountain of paperwork on his desk that has been building because of the many distractions caused by my cancer.

Mom is sitting at the kitchen table in her floral bathrobe and pink slippers when Pierre goes downstairs for coffee.

"I don't know what to do," she says.

"What do you mean?" Pierre asks.

"I don't know whether to take her up a cup of coffee. What if she's not awake?" Mom looks confused.

"Well, she's still asleep right now, but in a little while you could take a cup up and if she's sleeping you can just bring it back down. It's not a big deal."

Mom fidgets with her napkin. "I just want to do the right thing," she says. The little girl she has given birth to and raised is in a battle for her life, a battle her own husband lost. She is confused, as if she is not capable of doing much of anything.

"It's OK, Mom," Pierre says. "We just appreciate your being here with Judy.

Mom looks up and starts to cry. Pierre looks her in the eyes and sternly says, "Mom, you can't do that now. You are here to help Judy get through this. We need you to be strong while you are here. If you can't, I am going to put you on the next plane home."

Mom lifts her shaking hands to her mouth, nods her head. It is the last tear she sheds while she is in the house. She becomes the active caregiver I need.

Pierre and I stand in our bathroom with the door closed. I am naked. He pulls at the tape slowly and carefully, so he won't disturb the stitches, and removes the soiled bandages. Together we look at the new breast. It is a mound similar to a real breast with an angry looking four-inch horizontal scar where the nipple used to be. The nipple reconstruction comes last.

Every day for the rest of my life I will step out of the shower, look in the mirror, and see this odd breast with the scar. Every time I undress in front of my husband for the rest of our lives, he will see it. I study Pierre's placid face.

"Are you grossed out?" I ask.

"I wouldn't care if you had a concave chest," he says. He pulls me to him and gently wraps his arms around me. "All I want is you."

We are eating dinner when Dr. Benitez calls with my pathology report. The news is mixed—three out of eight lymph nodes have cancer. That is a pretty good ratio, but any cancer in the lymphatic system means more chemotherapy on top of radiation. That is bad news.

Generally, once cancer has spread to the lymph nodes, doctors will not pronounce you cured for five years after the treatments. Any cancer after the five-year period is considered new, not a recurrence of the original cancer.

I don't take time to feel sorry for myself. I want Mom to drive me to Bible study because I want her to hear the lecture on the call of Abraham. We leave immediately, and we don't say much on the way, but I'm thinking about the lymph nodes that mean the cancer could now be anywhere in my body.

It is late in the afternoon. A gray cast is spreading over the family room, but I don't get up to turn on the lights. Mom and I sit across from each other talking about my many cousins when she suddenly says, "Sometimes I feel like you don't want to have a relationship with me."

I am silent for a while, then I say, "We've never really had a very good one."

"Why is that?"

"Well, personally I think that was your responsibility, Mom."

She is defensive. "I'm close to Rick and Cindy. They call me all the time to confide in me and get my advice. I feel like I hardly know you."

"Mom, the three of you are all cut from the same cloth. I'm not like you. You never took the time to know me."

She is quiet.

"It has always been this way, Mom. You have never been able to affirm me for who I am."

"How can you say that?"

"I'm never good enough for you."

She looks confused. "What do you mean?"

"Are you aware that in forty-six years you have never once told me I was pretty?

She is visibly agitated. "That's ridiculous. Of course I've said you were pretty."

"Mom, do you know what you told me on my wedding day?"

"I said, 'You look beautiful.'"

"No, Mom, you said, 'You look nice.'"

She is speechless. We are both silent. The strain that has built all these years adds its own grayness to the fading light of the late afternoon. We both want the tension in our relationship to go away, but a lifetime of patterns and hurts litters the room between us.

Then she says, "Well, I've always thought you were beautiful. I've told everybody you were beautiful."

"Mom, you never once told me."

Her eyes well up with tears. "I think you are beautiful," she says, "inside and out."

My mother gives me her blessing. It is a moment that has taken forty-six years to arrive.

"You will surely forget your trouble,

recalling it only as waters gone by.

Life will be brighter than noonday,

and darkness will become like morning."

Job 11:16–17

My body heals quickly. Dr. Sherbert removes the drains and their plastic tubing. I throw away the pain pills. But healing exceeds the physical realm. It is cancer with all its ravages that begins mending my relationship with my mother. She needs to see me through this horrific reality of losing my breast and know that I can still be whole. And I need to see just how much she loves me. I find the evidence, not just in the words she is able, at last, to say to me, but even in her confusion over the small things like delivering coffee. She is confused because life is out of order. The child is not supposed to get cancer before the parent. I see in her face, in her inability to make decisions, in her desire to make me better, just how much she really does love me.

Pierre drives Mom to the airport.

She asks him, "What do you think is going to happen?"

Pierre is quiet a long time, then says, "Mom, Judy is going to die."

Mom's eyes fill up with tears.

Pierre continues, "Mom, I'm going to die, you're going to die, we're all going to die. Today, we're doing everything in our power to keep Judy from dying right now. We've selected the best doctors we can find, we've agreed to the most aggressive treatment possible, and we have thousands of people calling on the power of God. But there are no guarantees for her. There are no guarantees for any of us. Let's be thankful we have today."

JOURNEY SURVIVAL GUIDE

"And we know that in all things God works for the good of those who love him, who have been called according to his purpose" (Romans 8:28). Not all things are good, but in all things, even cancer, God can bring good. My oncologist once told me that many of his patients have told him cancer was the best thing that ever happened to them. While I won't go that far, it was cancer that began the healing process in my relationship with my mother. And the truth is, none of us knows how much longer we have, for it is God who determines our days. Cancer can teach us to value our days.

Teach us to number our days aright,
that we may gain a heart of wisdom.
Psalm 90:12

Seven

VALENTINE'S DAZE

Be merciful to me, LORD, for I am faint;
O LORD, heal me, for my bones are in agony.
My soul is in anguish.
How long, O LORD, how long?
—◦ PSALM 6:2–3 ◦—

Some days it is hard to remember that the doctors who are making me feel so bad are the good guys. There is a short break from treatment while my body heals from the mastectomy, then just days after Christmas chemotherapy starts again. This time it's Taxol. The side effects of this one are bone pain, which, Dr. Decker assures me, most patients prefer over the nausea caused by the Adriamycin and Cytoxan I previously received. And there is Decadron, a steroid, available to ease the bone pain.

The routine is the same, the lounge chairs in the chemotherapy room, the drip. Now I am accustomed to the routine and insist that Pierre go to the office. JoAnne Hazel drives me to chemo. She offers to stay with me, but I wave her on. This is going to be cake compared to previous cycles.

⚹   ⚹   ⚹

It is Monday. I am sitting at my desk at work. Every bone in my body aches. Even my skull aches. I walk like an old woman because the bones in my hips and legs hurt. I take the steroids, but I still have to ask the artists to come to my office. I move as little as possible. My face aches. I think of the old joke, "Does your face hurt? It's killing me." My face is killing me.

⚹   ⚹   ⚹

The steroids make my face swell, too. I feel uglier than ever. I solve this the way any true-blooded American woman would solve most any problem. I go shopping.

I start at the optical store. I try on glasses, pick out the pair I like the most without looking at the price, and write out a hefty check without wincing.

In a few days, I decide I need a new coat that will cover even my longest skirts. That means a coat that hangs all the way to my ankles and eliminates more than 99 percent of all coats, since I am five feet nine inches tall.

I start at the top. Neiman Marcus. The salespeople ignore me while I try on coats that cost more than my car is worth. But I don't find what I am looking for anyway. At Saks Fifth Avenue a saleswoman takes me seriously and brings me several long coats to try on. The only one long enough to cover the long skirt I am wearing costs a thousand dollars and looks just like a bathrobe.

I work my way along the mall slowly, walking like an old woman because every bone in my body aches, but the steroids make me feel powerful even though I walk funny. I search the stores. I know my coat is out there waiting for me somewhere.

In each store I push the coats around on their chrome carousels. Hold them up to my shoulders to see the length, try on the long ones. Put them back. Finally, I find the perfect coat—a long, black, soft wool coat that is so versatile I can easily wear it for black tie or with blue jeans. I take it to the cash register and hand the clerk my credit card. It is one of the most expensive brands in the store. Still, I feel I deserve it after all I've been through.

I don't realize that I am trying to solve the problems I am facing the way my own industry, advertising, tells us to fix them, with material things. Buying new things to improve my looks gives me temporary satisfaction.

I am on a roll. Now my house needs some sprucing up. I want furniture for the dining room.

I find it in the classified ads. "Mahogany Chippendale table with eight chairs." It is exactly what I want. It is used, which proves I am very frugal. I call the number listed.

A man answers the phone. "Yes, it's still available," he says, "but I'm getting a lot of calls. If you really want it, you better come today."

This is urgent. I tell him I will come straight from work and he gives me directions. I call Pierre to see if he wants to meet me, and he tells me he will "trust my judgment." It is a moment he will regret. He has lapses of memory and forgets I am on drugs.

After work I drive to the address, which turns out to be within a mini-warehouse park. I find the door with the right number on it and park. The door is locked. I knock, and the young man I spoke to on the phone answers.

"Please wait outside while I put the dogs away," he says. Then he adds, "Two Dobermans." He closes the door again. I stand outside in the dark. I don't hear any noise at all, and when he finally lets me in I don't hear any barking nor detect any doggie smell.

In the warehouse, the light is so dim I can barely see, but finally I spot my table and chairs right in the center of the room full of antiques and used furniture. I walk around the set, look under the chairs for a manufacturer's name but find none. I sit on one of the chairs. It seems comfortable enough.

"It's beautiful, isn't it?" he says.

"It might be a little too much for us," I say.

Then I tell him I am a cancer patient to win his sympathy. I don't like to give in to the temptation to use my disease to gain an advantage often. It's a card I save for special occasions. And this is one of them.

"My sister had breast cancer," he says.

"Oh, really?" This is more than I'd hoped for. "How is she doing?"

"Great," he says. "But it was a tough year."

I offer him five hundred dollars less than he is asking.

"I don't know," he says, looking worried. "I'll have to call my partner."

He makes a call on his cell phone.

"Hi, it's me," he says. "Look, I have a lady who wants the Chippendale set, but she's offering five hundred dollars less. She's a cancer patient—what do you say?"

He is silent a moment.

"How much do we have into it?"

I can't put my finger on it, but I have the funny feeling that there is no one on the other end of the line.

"OK," he says. He hangs up.

"She agreed," he says, "since you're a cancer patient."

I want the furniture delivered Friday afternoon when I know I'm going to be home from chemotherapy. He tells me it can only be delivered after 6:00 P.M. I don't realize until later that they don't want me to see it in the bright sunlight.

On Friday after my second round of Taxol, the young man and a woman who appears to be his wife arrive in a small truck and carry the table and chairs into the house. They set up the table with both leaves in my dining room. They carefully place six of the chairs around it and put the remaining two chairs in the corners of the room.

"It's perfect," the man gushes. "It just makes this room. And you got a great price."

"OK," I say, writing out the check. "Let's just hope the chairs don't collapse the first time we use them." I grin.

The man and the woman exchange glances.

It is truly an absurd thing for me to say, especially since it isn't until the second time we use them that Truett rocks back in his chair and it splits apart.

When I start looking at new cars with eight-hundred dollar monthly payments, Pierre finally figures out that the drugs are sending me into a shopping frenzy that is out of control, and he firmly reels me in like a snagged fish.

While you are undergoing cancer treatments it is dangerous to make any serious decisions such as a major purchase, a job change, or a move. Put major decisions on hold until the treatments are completed.

☧   ☧   ☧

It is Saturday. All my bones ache. I have taken the maximum dosage of steroids. My body is revved up as if I am on speed. Pierre comes into the kitchen from the garage and finds me sitting on the kitchen floor wearing rubber gloves and surrounded by every pot, pan, dish, colander, and sifter we own. An array of cleaning sprays, sponges, and rags is everywhere.

"What's going on?" he asks.

"I'm cleaning this filthy house."

"Let's get somebody else to help you," he says. "You shouldn't be doing this."

"Well, I should be making some kind of contribution to the family."

I am more than cleaning. I am in a full delirium, pulling things out of the cabinets and scrubbing the shelves out. I collect large garbage bags full of things to give away. I move in jerky motions with all my bones aching, but I am a woman with a mission. I work fast. In only a few hours I clean my entire kitchen from top to bottom. I survey the results and am satisfied.

I am fueled by the fact that I actually feel like doing something useful for a change and pumped to the max on steroids. I go upstairs to my closet. I start by taking everything out of it and dumping all my clothes, shoes, purses, and accessories onto the floor of our bedroom. Then I hang up all the things I wear on a regular basis. A friend told me this is what you are supposed to do. These are the "A" clothes. Everything else should be mended, altered, ironed, or thrown away. My closet is nearly empty. My bedroom is so littered with clothing you can't see the floor.

Pierre comes upstairs. "Man, the kitchen looks great," he says, "Now what are you doing?"

"I'm getting rid of all those clothes." I point to 75 percent of my wardrobe still on the bedroom floor.

"You can't throw all this away." Pierre looks frantic.

"This is why I can't figure out what to wear to work in the morning. I don't have enough 'A' clothes."

"What are you talking about?" Pierre asks, looking bewildered.

"My closet is jammed with all these clothes so I can't even see the clothes I actually want to wear."

"But this is all good stuff."

"I never wear it."

I limp downstairs holding onto the handrail and get a whole box of big black garbage bags. I limp back up the stairs and start stuffing the bags with my clothes. Pierre is lying on the bed.

"Wait," he says. "You've got some really good things here."

"Show me one thing."

He gets up and pulls out a Ralph Lauren denim skirt.

"Too tight."

"Try it on," he says.

I slip on the skirt. It fits perfectly.

"That's only because I have cancer."

"You can still wear it. And here, keep the black one too." He pulls the black denim skirt out of the garbage bag and clips both the skirts on hangers.

I keep stuffing the clothing into the bags. Pierre keeps pulling things out.

"What about this blouse? I love this on you." He holds up a red silk blouse.

"Too bright." I grab it from him and stuff it back into the bag.

I am a woman possessed. I bag up the clothes, tie the tops of the bags with plastic twisters and put them all on the front porch.

On Monday, the Veterans come and pick up all the bags. I will never see my clothes again.

$$\times \qquad \times \qquad \times$$

It is the Friday of Parents' Weekend at the University of Tennessee, and Lance is expecting us late tonight.

I am in my office at work, and in addition to aching all over, now I can't inhale fully. I call Dr. Decker's office and tell his nurse I have shortness of breath. She tells me to go to the hospital to have a chest X-ray. I might have pneumonia. I know Dr. Decker doesn't want me to go on the trip since I am in the middle of my chemo cycle and my immune system is low. It is Lance's Parents' Weekend, and I am his mother. I am going.

"We have to rule out pneumonia before you leave," his nurse tells me. "We'll get a wet reading of the X-ray right away. If everything is OK, you can still go."

I leave work and drive to the hospital. The X-ray is taken at the outpatient lab. I wait for the staff doctor to do the wet reading of the X-ray.

"I think you have pneumonia," he says. He calls Dr. Decker's office and instructs me to go to Emergency.

It is now late afternoon. I call Pierre. In an attempt to ward off another Emergency fiasco, Pierre calls the church to get prayer started. We can still make our 9:00 P.M. flight if I get a clean bill of health. Pierre meets me at Emergency.

A nurse escorts me to a private room and hands me a hospital gown. I am wheeled on a gurney down the hall for another chest X-ray. Then taken back to my room.

The physician-in-charge asks me to cough up phlegm into a Kleenex. She examines it. You know your life has deteriorated when the color of your mucus is of great interest to people.

A nice young man wearing green scrubs pushes a cart into the room.

"You're going to hate me," he says. "But I have to draw a lot of blood. They are going to do a lot of tests."

He's not kidding. He wraps an elastic band around my upper arm and sticks a needle in the crook of my elbow. I turn my head away while he draws blood. He fills vial after vial. Then he releases the elastic band. I feel dizzy when I see all the vials full of my blood.

"It's going to be awhile," he says. "Just sit tight." He pushes his cart out of the room. The vials containing my blood rattle.

I sit tight on the gurney while Pierre goes to the phone to see if we can get a later flight. There is nothing available, so he returns and paces as we watch the hands of the clock on the wall move around and around. Finally we know it is too late to make our flight. Parents' Weekend is one more thing we lose to cancer.

The physician-in-charge comes back into the room, smiling. "Your X-rays are normal," she says. "Your blood work is normal. You don't have pneumonia. We looked for signs of a blood clot. There are none. You can go home. Everything is normal."

"Normal?" I croak. "What do you mean normal?" I sit straight up on the gurney. "I had an X-ray this afternoon that showed I have pneumonia. I'm supposed to be on an airplane right now. I'm missing Parents' Weekend." I move closer to the doctor. "It better not be normal."

That is when Pierre gently puts his hand on my shoulder and quietly says, "Judy, isn't that what the church is praying for right now—normal?"

Pierre's gentle words pierce me through the heart. I am not even expecting God to be at work. I forget that "the prayer offered in faith will make the sick person well; the Lord will raise him up. . . . The prayer of a righteous man is powerful and effective" (James 5:15–16).

I have my third round of Taxol. The steroids make my face swell even more. I look like a sausage. For the next few weeks I feel as if every nerve in my body is exposed.

Pierre is having heart palpitations and goes to the cardiologist. He is exhausted. He works all day and comes home to do all the work we used to share. He cooks and cleans up. He does the laundry. He plans the meals. He buys the groceries. All I can do after a day of work is collapse. Truett is getting overlooked. Howard also correctly suspects that Pierre is struggling with depression.

I feel sorry for Pierre. Still, the old adage that misery loves company is certainly true in my case. Until now, I have worked hard to keep everyone around me from feeling miserable by trying to look normal and by staying "up" as much as possible. Now, for some reason, I bring Pierre into my inner circle of misery. I tell him of every ache, every wish to just go ahead and die. I loathe myself for adding to his misery, but as I said, misery loves company. And anyway, Pierre is barely listening.

I know that he wants to drop out of the battle; he seems to have been out of it emotionally for the last month. In the seven months since July he seems to have aged a hundred years. His business is slipping. He has gained thirty pounds from the stress. He looks like a confused, frustrated, foot-shuffling old man.

The cancer treatments continue and the fight gets harder; we are all worn out. But I have no choice but to press on. I feel totally alone now.

In our study of Genesis at BSF we are considering Abraham's sin in chapter 20 when, instead of admitting Sarah is his wife, which she is, he says she's his sister (she is his half-sister) to keep himself from being killed. This puts Sarah in peril in the household of Abimelech, king of Gerar.

Our teaching leader gives a lecture on the problem of "runaway imaginings." This, she says, is Abraham's problem. He lets his imagination take over, thinking of all the bad things that could happen instead of trusting God to protect them when they pass through Gerar.

"We do this, too," she says, "when we do not 'take every thought captive,' as we are instructed in 2 Corinthians 10:5. When we allow our imaginations to rule, we set ourselves up for sin."

It is only days before I become like Abraham myself, with runaway imaginings and sin of my own.

＊　　　＊　　　＊

I am sitting high up on the end of a table that is draped in white paper. I am wearing an examination gown and my blue jeans. A doctor walks towards me, reaches both hands upward, and I expect him to feel the lymph nodes at the base of my neck. Instead, he reaches behind my neck and unties the gown, slips it forward off my shoulders to reveal my breasts. "Let's see what's going on," he says. I sit perfectly still, cringing while he looks at my surgically damaged breast, now pumped up with saline. It is temporarily about the size of a bowling ball and just as soft.

"It looks good," he says. I know he is just trying to make me feel better about it, but I feel humiliated anyway. He pulls out an extension of the table for my legs, and I lie back.

"My stomach is suddenly protruding," I tell him.

He unzips my jeans and mashes my abdomen with his fingers feeling for anything unusual.

"It's probably the steroids," he says. "Sometimes that happens."

Nothing inappropriate occurs in the examination room. But within days something inappropriate begins to happen in my own head, as my runaway imaginings bring the scene back again and again. The doctor walks toward me, reaches behind my neck, unties my gown and slips it forward off my shoulders. He unzips my jeans. My writer's imagination takes over, and each version becomes more erotic in my drug-crazed head than the one before.

Paul warns:

> For though we live in the world, we do not wage war as the world does. The weapons we fight with are not the weapons of the world. On the contrary, they have divine power to demolish strongholds. We demolish arguments and every pretension that sets itself up against the knowledge of God, and we take captive every thought to make it obedient to Christ. (2 Corinthians 10:3–5)

There is a dangerous intimacy that develops with doctors to whom you entrust your life, who have seen you partially naked, disfigured, and try to make you feel good about yourself anyway. This intimacy, combined with what is known in the medical community as "transference," when a patient shifts the fulfillment of needs onto the doctor, offers great potential for trouble.

It is the first time in years that I have had such a strong reaction to a man who is not my husband. My mind is cruel, bringing the scene to life again and again and then mocking me with the absurdity that anyone would ever find me physically interesting again.

It is very common for women to have affairs after a mastectomy to reassure themselves that they are still appealing. I am not surprised. For months I have looked in the mirror and seen a woman I don't really recognize. My body is wrecked. I am not a beautiful woman. There are many women more beautiful, but I always looked better naked than most of them. The reality hits me that I am never going to look great naked again.

Perhaps at forty-six I should already have faced that reality. But I haven't. Perhaps I should also have taken more seriously Paul's imperative to "live by the Spirit, and you will not gratify the desires of the sinful nature" (Galatians 5:16).

It is Valentine's Day. I have bought Pierre a shirt and a fancy wooden tray for reading in bed. He opens his presents in the morning while I am still in bed, and there are tears in his eyes when he kisses me good-bye. He is leaving early for a business trip to Atlanta where he will be staying with my sister, Cindi. He doesn't give me any present. I go back to sleep, disappointed.

Pierre is one of thousands of American men who are fairly certain that Valentine's Day is a conspiracy against them. I don't know why in twenty-five years I have not learned to lower my expectations, but I don't. Every year I expect diamonds and receive instead something like a vase of flowers bought at the last minute because he either didn't plan ahead or is afraid to buy something I'll return.

When I wake up again I discover a dozen red roses in a vase on my dressing table, without a note. In my mind, the lack of a note of any kind confirms my suspicions that I am now a full-fledged freak, not worth any effort on Pierre's part.

I am hurt by Pierre's lack of planning and pumped up by steroids so everything is amplified. All day my anger stews. Why has he scheduled himself out of town on Valentine's Day? Why couldn't he be extravagant this year of all years?

I pack the wooden tray back in its box. I storm back to the store and return it, "ungifting" him without his knowledge. I rationalize that it's an old man's gift anyway and he is *not* going to turn into an old man yet.

After dinner I call Cindi's house.

"Happy Valentine's Day," she says cheerily.

"Oh really?" I snap back.

"What's wrong?"

"First, I have to spend it alone. Second, he bought me flowers at the last minute."

"Uh-o-o-oh, maybe I should put him on," Cindy says, handing Pierre the phone.

"How's my valentine?" he says unsuspectingly.

"You have really taught me to hate this day."

"Didn't you see the flowers?"

"You couldn't think of anything more original? Could you not write a card? Couldn't you even stay in town for it?"

"I'm sorry," he says. He is quiet for a long time. "I've had a lot on my mind in the last few weeks." His voice is heavy. I can tell he wants to cry. "Quite frankly I've had so much to do on every front, I truly didn't give it much thought. I'm really sorry."

I start to cry on the phone. I wanted to hurt him, and now I hate myself for doing it.

Dr. Sherbert is examining my bowling ball breast. I say something ridiculous to him, I don't remember what, and he says to me, "That's the drugs talking."

The drugs are making me say and do things that are out of character. Or, perhaps they are simply amplifying things that are wrong with my character that I need to deal with spiritually. Right now though, I am not thinking very spiritually. On the drive home I find some comfort in the fact that at least I recognize that I am crazy. It doesn't keep me from acting crazy; it just means that I feel better about my crazy self.

I am in our bathroom getting ready for bed. I look in the mirror at my naked body. I have one breast and one bowling ball.

My abdomen protrudes from the steroids. My swollen face is a sausage. I have a wild look in my eyes. The rest of me is an emaciated twig of a woman with a head so bald it shines in the overhead light. I put on my pajamas and open the bathroom door. I see Pierre propped up on pillows in the dark bedroom. I walk like an old woman to my dressing area, brush my teeth, wash my face. I can feel his eyes watching me the whole time. When I am ready for bed I look at him looking at me. There is enough light for me to see the expression on his face. I will never forget it. It says everything that I need to hear. It says everything about our marriage that has survived twenty-five years of for better and for worse, for richer and for poorer, in sickness and in health. On Pierre's expectant face I see that in his eyes my being alive makes me the most beautiful woman in the world and he can't wait for me to get in that bed with him.

In all of my life, it is the closest thing to unconditional love I have ever experienced from a human being. I slip into bed and move into his arms, longing for the day when Pierre can hold me without something hurting.

JOURNEY SURVIVAL GUIDE

Cancer is hard on the patient. It is also hard on the caregiver. For Christians, the husband knows that if his wife dies, she goes to be with the Lord, but he will be left alone. In the busy schedule of treatments and doctor visits, the physical and emotional ups and downs, it is easy for a cancer patient to take the caregiver for granted. Yet a good one, such as a faithful husband, is truly a gift from God.

*Love is patient, love is kind. It does
not envy, it does not boast, it is not
proud. It is not rude, it is not self-
seeking, it is not easily angered, it
keeps no record of wrongs. Love does
not delight in evil but rejoices with the
truth. It always protects, always trusts,
always hopes, always perseveres.
Love never fails.*

1 Corinthians 13:4–8

Eight

NUKE ME TILL I GLOW

Now for a little while you may have had to suffer grief in all kinds of trials.
These have come so that your faith—of greater worth than gold,
which perishes even though refined by fire—may be proved genuine
and may result in praise, glory and honor when Jesus Christ is revealed.

—◦ 1 PETER 1:6–7 ◦—

E arly in my cancer journey, my mother-in-law mentioned to Pierre that the time would probably come when I could no longer pray for myself. "It is the prayers of others that will carry her through the hardest time," she said.

I am there. My days are consumed with treatments and work. My thoughts are consumed with beating cancer and staying alive. I depend on the thousands of people who I know are praying. I also trust in the words of the apostle Paul, who says, "The Spirit helps us in our weakness. We do not know what we ought to pray for, but the Spirit himself intercedes for us with groans that words cannot express" (Romans 8:26).

There must be a lot of groaning going up from this body of mine.

I have chosen to take my radiation treatments simultaneously with the Taxol chemotherapy, for the convenience of my employers.

So while I am still crazy on Taxol and steroids, I begin my thirty days of radiation.

My temporarily reconstructed breast that is going to be radiated looks and feels enormous to me. I suspect that one of the reasons for the tissue expander is to make any reconstruction that follows such an improvement that the patient is automatically thrilled.

My radiation oncologist, Dr. Stromberg, shows me a video that explains exactly what to expect and the variations that can occur in skin damage. I am confident that I will fall into the category of "little damage." The receptionist gives me an appointment for something called the "simulation," an identification card, and a card that allows me to enter the parking garage with the doctors so I don't have to pay every day.

Pierre offers to go with me to the simulation.

"It's nothing," I tell him. A mistake.

When I arrive for the simulation I undress from the waist up and put on a hospital gown. An escort leads me down a hospital corridor to a large room filled with high-tech machinery. It is immediately obvious that this is a sophisticated business.

Two female technicians greet me and ask me to remove my gown. I don't want to undress in front of strangers in this big open room, but they aren't giving me a choice. One of them holds up a green towel, smaller than a dishtowel, in front of my breasts while I take off my gown. I don't want anyone to see my odd breast. I clutch the towel to my chest and they direct me to climb up on a table lined with white paper. First, they will make a mold of my head and arm that will be used during the actual radiation. When I lie down they realize I am wearing a wig and ask me to take it off so they won't ruin it. I don't want to take my wig off in front of strangers either, but again they aren't giving me any choice. I take it off and toss it onto a nearby chair. Now I am bald, half-naked, and totally humiliated.

For the mold, I lie down on my back into a form from my shoulders up. The form is filled with soft material that will harden within a few minutes. With one hand I hold the small towel across my breasts. The arm on the side to be radiated is curled around my head in the mold so that my side and armpit are completely exposed. Within a few minutes the mold hardens, and they remove it. A final plastic mold will be created and used during every one of my thirty radiation treatments to ensure that I am always in the exact same position. Precision in radiation is vital.

For the simulation itself I lie on a robotic table in the center of this huge room, shivering with cold. The technicians move the small towel and drape it across my good breast. My big ugly bowling ball breast is exposed for all the world to see, and I am aware that the technicians in the room aren't the only people present. Other technicians and Dr. Stromberg work in a dark adjacent room behind a glass window.

My two technicians roll my table around on its wheels and line me up with special lights. Overhead a large machine takes X-rays. Behind the glass window, Dr. Stromberg and the other technicians map out the exact field where radiation should occur so that it can enter and exit my body like invisible bullets from various angles, killing cancer cells without damaging my heart or lungs. There is no guessing.

The two technicians measure my big breast with a ruler, line me up, measure again. They mark on my naked body with felt tipped pens. Line me up differently, measure again, mark again. Over and over.

While they work, the technicians talk to each other as if I'm not present. They discuss their plans for the weekend. I realize I can't make any plans for the weekend because I'm having chemo on Friday and I don't yet know how I'm going to react. I think of all the weekends I have spent lying on the couch, and I feel sorry for myself.

One technician thinks she's funny. She cracks herself up with jokes about marking on my body.

I tell her I'm cold.

"You should have told us before," she says. "We wouldn't do

a thing about it, but we would like to know." She laughs. I don't, and I'm beginning to feel very upset.

Once the measuring and marking is finalized, it is time to tattoo me with tiny permanent dots to mark the area that will be radiated. They prick me with needles that feel like bee stings and add blue dye to fill the holes. The tattoos are miniscule, but the process takes nearly a half hour during which I have to lie with my arm crooked around my head in an uncomfortable position. The tattoos are the final insult. I don't want these permanent marks on my body no matter how small they are. I can't stop the tears that come.

If I had it to do over, I would take Pierre with me. When friends and loved ones offer to go with you to treatments and appointments, consider accepting. They might not be able to go into the room with you, but they can offer comfort for the ride home.

And, although I didn't want them, I discovered it is much better to have the tattoos than to risk having markings that could rub off. Radiation must be exact. Although the tattoos are permanent, they are so tiny that within months I could not find mine.

I sit at the kitchen table with Trevor. He is home from college for a weekend and is eating a bowl of cereal for breakfast. Then, he tells me, he will go shopping with his friend Caroline.

As I sit eating my own breakfast, it strikes me how simple life is when you are young. You wake up in the morning, and the day unfolds like a flower. But once something terrible happens to you, like cancer, days never unfold in quite the same way again.

This is one reason why God's people are so important on the journey. Faithful friends help us get our eyes off ourselves and back on Jesus. He is our true hope, both for physical healing and, if this is not His will, for ultimate healing. "A friend loves at all times, and a brother is born for adversity" (Proverbs 17:17). True friends remind us that Jesus promises:

"In my Father's house are many rooms. . . . I am going there to prepare a place for you. And if I go and prepare a place for you, I will come back and take you to be with me that you also may be where I am." (John 14:2–3)

It is Monday, my first day of actual radiation. I leave work at 3:00 and drive fast to make it to the hospital, park, and undress by 3:30. I enter the parking garage through the doctors' entrance. I pass their shiny, new cars on my way up the parking garage ramp to the patient parking where I park my twelve-year-old car.

I take the elevator to radiation, swipe my identification card across a device like a credit card swiper, and my name immediately appears on a TV screen overhead and alerts the technicians that I have arrived.

I go to the ladies' dressing room, and in a small booth I undress from the waist up and put on a hospital gown. I hang my clothes in a locker. While I am waiting, I sit in a chair in the dressing room, staring at but not really seeing the television that hangs from the ceiling. When my name is called I walk down the corridor to the radiation room, full of fear because I don't really know what to expect despite the film I watched.

Inside the large radiation room, two young women introduce themselves as my technicians. They are both warm to me, and I feel an immediate bond with them.

The routine is similar to the simulation. One technician holds up a small green towel while I take off my gown and hang it on a hook. This is intended to offer a semblance of modesty, but there is also a male technician in the room who does not speak and who does not have the courtesy to turn his head as I disrobe. I clutch the towel to my chest as I lie on the robotic table and the other technician places my mold under me. I raise my arm to curl around my head and situate myself into the mold.

There are red laser lights beaming down from the ceiling and from either side of the room. They raise the table several feet and move the towel to expose the breast to be radiated. There is no modesty now, even with a man in the room. The two women carefully line up my tattoos with the red lights. They push the radiation machine, which is suspended from the ceiling, into place over my body. It looks a little like an X-ray machine, only bigger, and has a lighted window on the bottom a few inches square with cross marks on it. They line up the marks according to the day's scheduled location for radiation and leave the room to watch from monitors in an office just outside the doorway. Now I am completely alone.

My job during radiation is to lie perfectly still, which means that every inch of my body immediately starts itching. Unlike the X-ray, the radiation machine loudly roars for about a minute. I can't feel anything happening. Then the technicians return, reposition the machine and leave again. The machine roars and I lie still, itching like crazy.

From Monday through Friday the routine is about the same, with the radiation machine pointing at me from different angles. After the first week I mention to Dr. Stromberg the male technician who watches me undress. The next week he is no longer present when I am.

Radiation becomes as much a part of my routine as brushing my teeth. If my technicians think I'm crazy from the drugs, they don't tell me. They always act glad to see me. They work hard to make an unbearable situation bearable.

Dr. Stromberg monitors my skin weekly. For about fifteen treatments it holds up well, looking slightly sunburned on my breast, under my armpit, and on my back where the radiation exits. She gives me cream to soothe the irritation.

Some days in the waiting room, there are other women wearing wigs and turbans sitting in the chairs waiting for radiation. Today the woman sitting next to me wants to tell me all her symptoms. She has lung cancer and coughs a lot while she talks. She's having a lot of problems from the radiation, although she didn't have to have chemo, thank God, so at least her hair hasn't fallen out. I feel bad that I don't want to hear about all her symptoms, but I don't. I want somebody to hear about mine.

Whining and complaining quickly wear out family and friends, and the last thing you want is isolation. Grumbling will not restore your health. Worst of all, it is displeasing to God. The Israelites continuously grumbled about their circumstances in the wilderness after their exodus from Egypt. "When the LORD heard them, he was very angry; . . . for they did not believe in God or trust in his deliverance" (Psalm 78:21–22). I learned to try to keep my medical complaints inside the doctors' offices and take my needs, fears, hurts, and desires directly to God, who is always available to listen.

I love the LORD, for he heard my voice;

he heard my cry for mercy.

Because he turned his ear to me,

I will call on him as long as I live.

Psalm 116:1–2

My name is called. I leave the dressing room and walk down the hall to sit on the bench outside the radiation room. An old man with a gray beard and vague eyes sunken in his grave face sits across from me. Out of the blue he says, "It's like sheep to the slaughter."

I am so surprised by this thoughtless comment to another cancer patient that I blurt, "Oh, I hope not. I'm planning to get well."

When I am called for my turn, I am still thinking about the old man's comment.

My cousin, a doctor, once said, "They don't call it the *practice* of medicine for nothing." Now, I wonder, are they just experimenting on me? Am I just a sheep to the slaughter?

I am lying on the radiation table when I hear an interesting song playing on the intercom, Eric Clapton's "My Father's Eyes."

I look up at the ceiling and realize that the two red laser lights are set in a circular indention that looks like a face. I begin to imagine that they are my Father's eyes. I know that I am a sheep but not for the slaughter, for I am a sheep of the Good Shepherd. I think about Him watching me, and I realize that I am not alone at all. I close my eyes while the machine roars and remember, "The eyes of the LORD are on the righteous and his ears are attentive to their cry" (Psalm 34:15).

At the hospital they are very good about maintaining my appointment times. In today's medical world this is extraordinarily rare and shows great respect for patients. I don't want to be the one to throw off the schedule. I only have a half-hour to arrive, park, and undress. The steroids make me feel bold and invincible. I drive fast. I change lanes too quickly. I cut people off. I have a vague sense that I should be more careful, but I am unconcerned that I am dangerous. On the days I drive Pierre's Blazer, I sit up high and feel even more invincible.

I mark off the days in my calendar. The weeks pass. I will

finish my thirty treatments soon. I'm glad, because my skin is beginning to look red and dried out, angry.

Some days they mark on my breast with a marker despite the tattoos and since there is no place to wash the markings off in the dressing room before I get dressed, I have ruined my clothes. My work wardrobe diminishes. I have already thrown out 75 percent of my clothes in a cleaning frenzy. I wear separates because I have to undress from the waist up. I am lopsided, ruling out anything clingy, and now black markers are causing problems.

After ruining two of my favorite bras and a creamy silk blouse, I become fond of black. For even with tattoos there are days when the technicians mark you with ink that washes off your skin but not your clothes.

I am lying in my four-poster bed at home. It is snowing outside, but my blouse is unbuttoned to reveal my bowling ball breast. It is draped in wet gauze. I was wrong to think I would be one of the lucky patients with minimal skin damage. I have some of the worst. My skin looks like it is about to burst into flames. Radiation is postponed. I can't go to work. Every few hours I have to lie down and drape my breast with gauze soaked in special solution to ease the damage to the inflamed skin and reduce the discomfort.

I try to read, but it is hard to concentrate. Suddenly my two forearms start throbbing, my hands tingle. They go numb. I wonder if this is what it feels like to die.

Dr. Stromberg resumes my treatments. I am lying on the radiation table just like every other day when the roaring machine goes dead too soon. Silence. I lie there itching, uncertain what to do. Nobody comes into the room, but over the intercom someone tells me to stay still, the power should come back up. We wait a long time. Then suddenly the radiation machine roars again.

Afterwards I sit up and ask, "What was that?"

"Oh, just a power surge," someone says.

Great, I think, *a power surge of radiation.* That should be good for me.

I have an appointment with Dr. Benitez that same day. The power is off at the parking garage so the wooden arm won't go up. I drive around the various buildings looking for parking. Every lot is full. I drive over to the hospital entrance to valet park.

Now I have to walk to the office building. It's probably not more than a hundred yards from my car, which would be no problem for a well person. But my body is so worn out by now and aching from the Taxol that it looks like miles, and it is getting ready to rain. The wind is gusting. I hold my purse and umbrella in one hand. I use my other hand to hold my hair on. It is the only day since I have been sick that I have worn high heels to work. By the time I finish limping to Dr. Benitez' office I can barely walk. I take the elevator up and sit in a chair in her waiting room.

With breast cancer it is not enough to feel like dying with every chemotherapy treatment. You look ugly. Your hair falls out. You get a gray pallor to your skin, a frantic look in your sunken eyes. And with radiation you can't wear deodorant of any kind. As I sit waiting for Dr. Benitez I realize that after that hike I smell bad too. It's all a package deal.

"So we fix our eyes not on what is seen, but on what is unseen. For what is seen is temporary, but what is unseen is eternal" (2 Corinthians 4:18). I am lying on the radiation table looking up and thinking of the eyes of God looking down on me.

The beam between us is red, and I ponder this. That's when it hits me like a power surge. He sees me through the blood of Christ. "In him we have redemption through his blood, the forgiveness of sins, in accordance with the riches of God's grace" (Ephesians 1:7). Jesus' blood can make even a drug-crazed, sinful, prayerless menace of a cancer patient like me look acceptable to God. It's a miracle I accept on faith but will never fully understand. He loves me. As the radiation machine roars, I close my eyes and thank Him.

Now I know that it really doesn't matter if I live or die of cancer because I have a God who has already met my ultimate need to be healed for eternity through the blood of Christ. He will raise me from the dead as surely as He raised Jesus Christ . . . to be with Him forever. I realize what Paul meant when he wrote, "For to me, to live is Christ and to die is gain" (Philippians 1:21). Although survival is certainly the goal, our ultimate finish line is Jesus. Staying focused on Him is the key to the journey. I think of the writer to the Hebrews, who says,

> Therefore, since we are surrounded by such a great cloud of witnesses, let us throw off everything that hinders and the sin that so easily entangles, and let us run with perseverance the race marked out for us. Let us fix our eyes on Jesus, the author and perfecter of our faith. (Hebrews 12:1–2)

Hopefully, when my time comes, I will be able to say with Paul, "I have finished the race, I have kept the faith" (2 Timothy 4:7).

My thirty treatments of radiation, which have taken nearly seven weeks, are over. My skin appears to be permanently damaged. Then, without warning, all the ruined skin peels off, and underneath a layer of fresh, new skin as soft as a baby's, emerges. It is not at all unlike the transforming work of the Spirit, as the old self is gradually yielded to the light of God's scrutiny and we are transformed into the beautiful image of Christ.

JOURNEY SURVIVAL GUIDE

Cancer is a roller-coaster ride, even for Christians. One minute we are full of faith and expecting miracles, the next we are overwhelmed with our physical needs and close to mental breakdown. Treatments are long and grueling. Cancer is no sprint. It's a marathon. We can wallow in self-pity or be overcomers—we choose what our minds dwell on. This is where having God's people in close contact, Scripture to call upon, and a spontaneous prayer life can make all the difference.

Do not conform any longer to the pattern of this world, but be transformed by the renewing of your mind. Then you will be able to test and approve what God's will is—his good, pleasing and perfect will.

Romans 12:2

Nine

CAR PAY DIEM

Of what use is money in the hand of a fool,
since he has no desire to get wisdom?

⟶ PROVERBS 17:16 ⟵

I am sitting high up on an examination table, which is lined with white paper. Today is my last chemotherapy treatment. I am wearing a pure white cotton gown and my blue jeans. Dr. Decker enters the room, wearing his white coat. He pulls a padded stool on wheels up close to me and sits down. I dig a list of questions from my blue jeans pocket, and he patiently answers them.

While I am asking the questions from my rumpled paper, I see Dr. Decker looking at me peculiarly, studying my face.

When I have finished with my questions he says, "You still have eyelashes and eyebrows."

I nod my head. "They are hanging in there."

He opens my file and studies a picture of me that was taken the first day I came to his office.

"You know, Judy," he says, "you don't look all that much different today than you did when you first walked in here."

I know what he means, because even though I feel ugly, I have seen the other cancer patients in his waiting room; many of them far more deteriorated than I am, some so sick they come in their pajamas, so gray they look barely alive.

I laugh and flippantly answer, "Oh, you know, a good wig and makeup, it's a miracle of modern science."

Dr. Decker is quiet. He slowly closes the file. He looks over his gold-rimmed glasses at me for a moment, and then he says softly, "No, Judy, I think you should consider it . . . a miracle."

I can think of nothing to say. I sit still waiting for Dr. Decker to make the next move. His words have cut me to the heart.

All these months since July I have been living Mach 2.0 with my hair on fire, enduring the intense cancer regimen of doctors' appointments and treatments, all the while working under the insane daily pressure of advertising deadlines. Through it all I have managed to look somewhat normal to others, and now I have taken the credit for it.

With this gentle word I know immediately that God is speaking to me once again, this time through Dr. Decker. It is God who is sustaining me, and I have not given Him the glory He is due, for He says, "I will not yield my glory to another" (Isaiah 48:11).

I vow inwardly that this will not happen again.

After my exam with Dr. Decker, I sit in a brown vinyl lounge chair in the chemotherapy room for my final treatment. Several hours later, after the last drop has dripped through the plastic tubes and into my body, I awake to see Pierre sitting across from me waiting to drive me home. Several nurses walk over and stand in front of me with their arms extended, their hands in fists. They toss bright pieces of confetti on me to celebrate the end of my treatments, so that my wig and my clothes are covered with tiny colored bits of paper. They hug me.

It is a celebration for all of us. For me, because finally I have had the last dose of chemotherapy and within a month or two I can begin feeling something like normal again. For the nurses, because their work has resulted in a living, breathing cancer survivor.

To be sure, while in every case you hope that victory is attainable, that is simply not always the case.

But in my case, nevertheless, today is a victory. I walk out on wobbly legs, a one-woman ticker-tape parade. Tiny bits of confetti litter the floor on my way down the corridor. I see Dr. Decker in his white coat standing in the main office, looking through a file. I stop at the doorway and wave good-bye to him. A chapter in my life is coming to an end. I am going to miss seeing him so regularly.

The effects of the last Taxol treatment and the accompanying steroids will last at least a month. My eyelashes and most of my eyebrows do eventually succumb to the drugs and fall out. I get that alien look I have dreaded, but I consider myself lucky for having to look that way for only a short time. I have a few eyebrows left so I can see where they belong and color them in with a special pencil. I wear a lot of eyeliner to make up for no eyelashes.

Although the drugs will do their damage to the bad cells and the good cells and take their time working all the way out of my body, psychologically I feel I am finished. Therefore, I decide to buy myself a new car to commemorate the occasion.

As I have already said, cancer counselors will tell you not to make any major decisions when you are dealing with a disease as traumatic as cancer. However, nobody tells me this, because I haven't been to a cancer counselor.

For several days I stop in at showrooms on my way home from work. I still want a spiffy car, but now I know that Pierre will not sign the papers with me unless I find one we can actually afford.

One evening, Pierre meets me at a dealership where a car on the showroom floor shines in the bright floodlights. It is a small, sporty model in a shade of blue the color of the ocean at South Beach in Miami. The price is right. It is the car for me.

A woman rushes over to point out all the features—sporty wheel covers, sunroof, leather interior, heated seats, CD player, and a tape deck. I play my cancer card for the second time to get the lowest price.

"Oh, honey," she says, "you deserve this car after all you've been through."

I couldn't agree with her more. I decide on the spot to buy the car. She offers me a "special discount," and we fill out the papers.

It will take a couple of days before the financing is finalized, and during that time Pierre and I discuss the wisdom of taking on another car payment.

"Well then," I say one night while we are cleaning up the kitchen after dinner, "let's put out a fleece."

Gideon said to God, "If you will save Israel by my hand as you have promised—look, I will place a wool fleece on the threshing floor. If there is dew only on the fleece and all the ground is dry, then I will know that you will save Israel by my hand, as you said." And that is what happened. Gideon rose early the next day; he squeezed the fleece and wrung out the dew—a bowlful of water.

Then Gideon said to God, "Do not be angry with me. Let me make just one more request. Allow me one more test with the fleece. This time make the fleece dry and the ground covered with dew." That night God did so. Only the fleece was dry; all the ground was covered with dew. (Judges 6:36–40)

I say to Pierre, "Let's say that if God does not want us to buy this car he will cause a problem with the financing. If not, we go ahead."

"I question the soundness of this theology," Pierre says. "But . . . OK. Let's see what happens."

The next morning I am sitting in front of my computer at work when the woman from the dealership calls me.

"We have a slight problem," she says.

"What's that?"

"The financing I quoted you was incorrect. It's going to be a quarter percent higher, but it hardly raises your payments." She tells me the amount.

I am quiet for a minute. I want this car. However, I realize this is the answer we prayed for. "I'm sorry," I say, "I'm going to back away from the deal. Perhaps we'll come back another time, but for now I'm going to back out."

She is flabbergasted that I would let the perfect car go for a tiny quarter percent interest. The difference in the payments is so negligible. I wish I had told her the real reason—this was God's answer—but I didn't.

Instead I call Pierre. "The deal's off." I tell him about the financing.

"I'm sorry," he says. "I know you wanted that car. But something better will come along."

After lunch my phone rings again. This time it is the manager of the dealership.

"We really want you to have this car," he says. "We can't do anything about the financing, the percentage you were quoted is unavailable. But we have decided to lower the price of the car so that your payments will be exactly what they were before."

I call Pierre again and tell him the offer. "So really," I rationalize, "it's a better deal because we usually pay the cars off early anyway. In the long run it will actually cost less."

He is quiet. Then he says, "We asked God to show us what He would have us do. We agreed to back away if there is any trouble with the financing. It seems to me that He has shown us what to do. But you do what you think is right. I'm with you whatever you do. I will trust your judgment." The poor man keeps forgetting that my judgment cannot be trusted.

I want the car. The "fleece" seems less black and white to me now and more of a pale shade of gray. I call the manager back and arrange to sign the final papers and pick up the car that very night.

Driving it home in the twilight, I sing loudly along with my new amazing stereo. I feel like a glorious woman again in my glorious new car.

$$X \qquad X \qquad X$$

I am celebrating the end of treatments. All that remains is the reconstruction, and that is happy surgery. Yet I start feeling as if all my nerves are always on edge, and there are times when my heart without warning starts beating so hard I am afraid I am going into cardiac arrest. I make an appointment with Dr. Decker's wife, Veronica, who provides cancer counseling.

When I arrive at her office, Veronica Decker escorts me back to a small room and has me sit in a Chippendale chair that reminds me of my dining room chairs, only sturdier. She sits across from me at a small computer desk. She is a petite woman with sandy-colored hair and a face that is pretty without makeup. She has a friendly manner that makes it easy to talk to her. We begin with my medical history from the time of the diagnosis to today. When I am finished, she says, "So you've worked and stayed strong throughout . . . for everybody else."

"For the most part."

"Judy," she says, "you haven't taken any time for yourself, to mourn, to rest, to heal."

"I thought it was better to keep working, to do normal things and not sit around feeling sorry for myself."

She says softly, "But it's been a horrible year."

I nod.

"What are you feeling about what you've been through?" she asks me.

I am quiet for a few seconds, then say, "Well, that's the weird thing. I'm not really very in touch with my feelings, which is unusual for me. I used to be pretty introspective."

She makes notes on a pad and says, "First we have to rule out heart problems, and I'm going to send you to a cardiologist, but I don't think that's what it is. I think you should try writing some thoughts in a journal. Try to get in touch with your feelings. Consider taking some time off from work to heal, to look at your life, to ask yourself if you are happy with your life, to get well."

As I drive home her words echo in my head, *Ask yourself if you are happy with your life, to get well.*

That weekend my good friend Candy Yocom flies in from Louisville, Kentucky, to visit me. Candy was my close friend when we lived in Charleston, when life was simpler and we had not yet been brutalized by it.

On Saturday, Candy and I ride around in my new car. Being with her now makes me remember the way life used to be. In an odd way it is as if no time has passed because Candy is one of those friends with whom time makes no difference. We pick our friendship back up just where we left it last time.

We shop the mall together. We try on clothes. We eat lunch at Neiman Marcus, drinking water with thin slices of lemon out of tall, deep blue goblets, sipping chicken consommé before our fancy lunches and splurging on crème brûlée for dessert. We catch up on the details of our lives.

Candy is one of those rare friends with whom I can be completely myself. I am so comfortable with her I can talk to her about everything from God to sex. Over coffee I confess to her about the runaway imaginings that I had over a doctor.

She laughs, her blue eyes twinkling. "You mean you lusted in your heart?"

"Yes, and it scares me."

Then she tells me of an experience she once had when she was going through a mid-life crisis. "I think every woman has that experience," she says matter-of-factly. "Confess it to God and get over it."

On Sunday morning I drive her to the airport, and we hug for a long time before she boards the airplane.

On Sunday afternoon after Candy has gone my heart starts beating too hard. My arms tingle. My hands go numb. Then I start to cry for no apparent reason and I cannot stop. I am crying so hard that I could not tell Pierre what is wrong even if I knew. He is bewildered. He has a meeting at church, and he asks if I want to be alone or have him stay. I tell him I want to be by myself. He goes. Truett leaves for youth group.

I am totally alone in the house and glad for it. While I am crying, I take out a pad of paper to begin journaling as Veronica has suggested, getting in touch with my feelings. I begin by writing down all the things I do not want to do.

> *I don't want to have something to do 24 hours a day.*
> *I don't want to wear a wig.*
> *I don't want to have to look good.*
> *I don't want to do laundry.*
> *I don't want to be around anyone who needs anything from me.*
> *I don't want to paint anything or fix anything else in this house.*

I fill up page after page.
Then I begin to write what I want to do.

> *I want to lie in a beach chair beside the ocean.*
> *I want to look beautiful in a bathing suit again.*
> *I want to read a book that I want to read.*
> *I want to be a writer with a project that is important,*
>   *if only to me.*
> *I want a friend like Candy here in Michigan.*

Then I write something that is very telling. *I want to stay home tomorrow and take care of myself but if I do that I won't have any vacation days left to have some fun. Life is no longer fun. Why has God taken all the fun out of my life? My house always has something broken. My body is broken. I am broken. My life is broken. Everything feels broken.*

I realize that I am now looking at my life as Veronica suggested, and I do not like what I see. I was happy with my life in Charleston. Yes, the house, the town, the time in our lives were all a part of it, but even more, I realize I am no longer the woman I was there—the reader, the deep thinker, the friend with time on her hands for relationships.

My life has become hurly-burly, going through the motions, moving too fast, living by a planner, pressed by deadlines, over-committed. Even the time I spend on my Bible study is rushed. There is no time for thinking, for longing, for just being. I realize to my horror that I have to stay in the hospital to do the things I love to do. I am no longer a human being, I am a human doing.

When Pierre comes home two hours later I am completely spent. My eyes are red and swollen, my face puffy, but I am able to tell him one thing. My life feels broken, and if I cannot get back to a life that is who I am at my core, then it is not worth getting out of bed for. There is no point in getting well.

"So let's take some time to consider our options," Pierre says.

On Monday I call the company chairman and request a leave of absence for four weeks, until one week after my reconstruction surgery.

"I need some time to get well," I say.

He agrees.

The cardiologist that Veronica Decker sends me to rules out heart damage. I have a strong athletic heart.

I spend my leave of absence reading books I have not had time to read while I was working; I start writing, not for paying clients, but for the joy of writing itself. I begin one project and abandon it for another until I have started and abandoned a dozen projects.

But I don't care. I am writing for the fun of writing. I am being me.

I go out to lunch with women I have wanted to be my friends. For these four weeks I don't have to sit at my desk at work and gulp down whatever leftovers I have happened to bring or a dry sandwich from the deli downstairs. I spend time cultivating relationships with women over long lunches in restaurants.

I am driving down the road in my car one evening at dusk when a sad song comes on the radio and my eyes fill up with tears. I am feeling the song from a place deep within me that hasn't been touched in a long time. That's when I realize that is the woman I am. Living my life with every minute scheduled leaves me no time to feel anything deeply, because to survive the kind of life I have been living, there is no time to feel much of anything at all. "Keep going" is my mantra. "Check off the next thing on the list." I know now it is no way for me to live.

At last, the day arrives for my reconstructive surgery. I am finally getting rid of the bowling ball and getting a silicone implant that will be softer and more like a real breast. The nipple reconstruction comes later. I am sitting in a private room at the hospital when Dr. Sherbert arrives. He asks me to stand beside the bed and lower my gown to my waist. Again, he marks on my body with a black marker to give himself perspective while I am lying down. He leaves to prepare for surgery.

A nurse comes into the room to hook my arm up to the IV drip. She says, "Dr. Sherbert is kind of new here, but he is the very best we have. You are so lucky to have him."

I know luck has nothing to do with it.

My reconstruction goes perfectly, and now the reality of having two sons in college means I have to go back to work. On Thursday afternoon I call my boss, the company chairman, to reassure him I'll be in on Monday as we discussed. He isn't in, so I leave a voice mail message. On Friday I am outside potting geraniums when Pierre brings me the portable phone. It is the company president.

"Why don't you just take the whole summer off and really get well," he says.

"I'm ready to get back to work," I say.

"You are much more important than this job."

"We need the income."

He stalls for a moment, then says, "We've got somebody else in your place."

"Excuse me?"

"Collect unemployment for the summer, then call us around Labor Day," he says flatly, "and we'll work something out."

I cannot believe what I am hearing. I have been a loyal employee. I worked through chemotherapy, scheduled my mastectomy to coincide with Thanksgiving holidays to minimize time off, never mind that it interfered with my holiday. I worked while having both radiation and chemotherapy simultaneously. I worked nauseated, wearing a wig all day to hide my baldness. I drove to work through nearly three feet of snow with all my bones throbbing. I met their deadlines.

Now I can't return.

I am caught completely off guard. This is the man who came into my office on numerous occasions during my illness saying, "Do whatever it takes to get well. This job is one thing you don't have to worry about."

Apparently I did.

I am mourning. We are feeling the devastating loss of my income. Unemployment compensation is only a fraction of my paycheck. In addition to our house payment and school loans for both older boys, we now have two hefty car payments. I hang on for several payments, but there is no way to carry on. My new car has to go. It is one of the few things that has been exciting to me in the past year, and now that is being taken away, too. I don't want to lose it.

Finally, after dinner one evening I decide to sell my car and find something less expensive.

The very next morning I am getting dressed when our friend Jim Hazel calls.

"Somebody told me you have a new car," he says. He names the model. "I'm thinking of buying one, and I want to see how you like yours."

"I love it," I say. "Want to buy mine?"

He laughs. I am silent.

"Are you kidding?" he asks.

"I wish I was."

"Why are you selling it?"

"Because I don't have a job, and I can't make the payments."

As it turns out, Jim is planning to buy my exact car.

"Well, maybe we can come up with something that is beneficial to both of us," he says.

He and Pierre meet for lunch. They settle on a price we can all live with. The car is sold as painlessly as possible.

Now I need a car. I haven't talked to my brother Rick in a while, but I feel compelled to call him. I remember a conversation we had months ago when he was considering selling his car.

"Are you still thinking about selling your car?" I ask him.

"I'm selling it next week."

"Will you sell it to me?"

"Of course."

I know my brother's car has high mileage, but I also know he has kept it in pristine condition. He gives me such a good price I can write a check for it.

Now I know why we had problems with the financing on my new car. We had put out a fleece to God and He answered, clearly showing us not to buy it. This was not because he was mean or didn't want me to have anything nice, but He knew the bigger picture. He knew in advance that I would lose my job, and He was trying to protect me from the heartache and embarrassment of having to sell it. "If only you had paid attention to my commands, your peace would have been like a river, your righteousness like the waves of the sea" (Isaiah 48:18).

I have to pay the consequences of my disobedience by selling my car and taking a loss. The Bible is clear: God disciplines us when we don't do things His way. As the writer to the Hebrews puts it, "Endure hardship as discipline; God is treating you as sons. For what son is not disciplined by his father?" (Hebrews 12:7). But also like a father, He eases the pain by providing both a buyer and another car. God is faithful to His children.

It is not a new car that I really need at this time in my life. What I need has nothing at all to do with the material possessions that have been luring me with their deceptive and transient pleasures. What I need is something far deeper, more permanent. What I need is what my Father in heaven wants to give me, more of his Holy Spirit in me, that is, more of Himself.

JOURNEY SURVIVAL GUIDE

Allow the cancer journey to be a time of examination. Are you happy with your life? Are your relationships in order? This is a good time to set things right. Pray for God to reveal the areas in your life that need to be changed, and use cancer as a springboard for doing it. However, sometimes when we are hurting we are tempted to hurry ahead of God in our attempts to ease the pain. When we do this, we run the risk of making things worse. If we can learn to wait on the Lord, He will meet all our needs with the perfect solution in the perfect time.

> *"If you then, though you are evil,*
> *know how to give good gifts to your*
> *children, how much more will your*
> *Father in heaven give the Holy Spirit*
> *to those who ask him!"*
>
> Luke 11:13

Ten
THE SPIRITUAL LIFE

In all these things we are more than conquerors through him who loved us.
For I am convinced that neither death nor life, neither angels nor demons,
neither the present nor the future, nor any powers, neither height nor depth,
nor anything else in all creation, will be able to separate us from
the love of God that is in Christ Jesus our Lord.

—◦ ROMANS 8:37–39 ◦—

There is, in a very real sense, the idea that all of life is prayer. For those of us who belong to God, the very world in which we live and move and have our being is a kind of prayer in and of itself. There is also the idea of praying without ceasing, and I think that this is at least a part of what it means when the Bible teaches that the Holy Spirit is interceding for us. But there is also the work of prayer. This is what Jesus demonstrated in His own life in the times when He went off alone to pray and is at least a part of what He was getting at when He rebuked His sleeping disciples at Gethsemane: "Could you men not keep watch with me for one hour?" (Matthew 26:40). This kind of prayer, even for Jesus Himself, is important work.

Because I have rested on the prayers of others for so many months, my own prayer life has become greatly impoverished. I have difficulty getting back into regular communication with God because so much has happened to distract me. As my cancer journey nears its end, I know that restoring my own prayer life—the uninterrupted time of seeking God in adoration, confession, thanksgiving, and supplication—is as important for the health of the rest of my life as defeating the cancer itself.

As I work on my prayer life, I remember a time early in my relationship with my friend Shellie Gay Bohannon. We were both rather new in Charleston, and for some reason, Shellie Gay, whom I barely knew, reached out to me more than anyone else did during a time when I was depressed over my father's death.

One day she calls and wants me to come to her home for lunch. I don't remember much about the lunch, what we eat or what we talk about. What I remember is her telling me that when she prays, she literally goes into a closet to get away from the distractions of family life.

It surprises me that anyone would actually do this, although Jesus Himself says, "When you pray, go into your room, close the door and pray to your Father, who is unseen. Then your Father, who sees what is done in secret, will reward you" (Matthew 6:6).

"You're kidding?" I say.

"I'm not," she says and leads me upstairs to show me.

It is her husband Mitchell's closet that she uses, and after she warns Jenni, her blond-haired preschooler, to leave us alone for a few minutes, the two of us go into the large closet together, close the door and turn off the light. We kneel facing each other on the carpeted floor holding hands in the dark. Mitchell's suits hang neatly in a row above us; the rich smell of his leather shoes and belts surrounds us. Shellie Gay begins to praise God, the words flowing from her mouth as if this is the most natural thing in the world for two friends to do after lunch, to go into a dark closet and pray. When it is my turn, I am so unnerved by the whole setting, having previously prayed fairly little in front of others, that I do little more than mumble a few awkward words. Shellie Gay saves the day by jumping in and concluding the prayer, asking God to take the depression away from me and fill the void with His Holy Spirit.

Afterwards, we sit on the end of the bed in the master bedroom. Jenni runs through the room with her blond hair flying back, jumps up on the bed, takes a few good bounces across it, jumps down on the other side, and is gone as quickly as she has arrived.

We discover that she has left something of significance, which she as a preschooler could have no way of understanding. She has dropped on the bed a small painted wooden dove, the traditional symbol for the presence of the Holy Spirit. Shellie Gay's brown eyes get wide, and I start to laugh. I haven't laughed much for many months, but I laugh now from somewhere deep down inside me. I laugh as I say good-bye to Shellie Gay. I laugh as I drive home. My depression begins lifting soon after, and laughter becomes a regular part of my life once again.

I think of that day in the closet with Shellie Gay as I work on the discipline of getting my prayer life back on track. I don't believe we need to go literally into a dark closet to pray, although it doesn't hurt our concentration. Surely we can pray anywhere—in a church pew, at the office, driving our car, stirring a pot of spaghetti. But Shellie Gay taught me something about getting serious with God in prayer. It is a work about which He is very serious. I have kept the small dove for fifteen years as a reminder.

Cancer has helped me to understand something of what it means when we Christians pray in Jesus' name. For most of my Christian life it has been something that I hastily tacked on at the end of my prayers—"I pray in Jesus' name"—because that is what Christians do. Through the cancer journey I begin to see that His name is not some kind of rabbit's foot that we rub to get what we want. There is power in His name, to be sure, but even more, as our lives triumph through prayer, we bring glory to Christ. Our praise through adversity, our faith that overcomes difficulty, draws attention to Jesus, even if the attention is only our own.

I learn to pray frequently and with renewed zest. I pray at church. I pray in my car. I pray stirring a pot of spaghetti. And every now and then I go into my own closet and kneel in the darkness.

X   X   X

I have no job for the summer, and money is tight. However, now my time with my sons is extravagant. They are all three home for the summer, working as lifeguards at a local country club. During their days off I have time to spend with them, time that is precious and fleeting, for they will all be leaving home for good in less time than I want to think about. Some days it is as if God moves all the right forces together so that they are open, and we have long talks about their futures, love, marriage, sex, their walk with Christ.

In the evenings, we cook out on the patio beside the pool and play island music, as if we are back in Miami where we lived prior to Michigan. On the green lawn in the backyard we play croquet, which the boys always complain about, but which we play anyway with great zeal because we are all so competitive.

One evening at dusk we are playing croquet when Lance thinks it will be funny to yank my chain. He comes outside wearing khaki shorts and a Hawaiian shirt, his legs brown and his feet bare. He makes a big production of lighting up an enormous cigar. I pretend not to notice. He makes several shots with both hands on the croquet mallet, the cigar firmly pressed between his lips. Then, because I have ignored him, he asks me to hold the cigar for him while he takes his next shot. I take the fat brown cigar from him and, with all the boys watching to see my reaction, I take a big drag on it, blow the smoke back toward Lance, and smile.

"Wait," Trevor yells, "it's a Kodak moment." He runs inside for a camera, runs back out and takes my picture. The boys all give me a look. It is a look I have seen before.

I saw it in Miami ten years ago when the boys were all Little Leaguers at the time. We had ridden our bikes from our home to Bayfront Park in Coconut Grove where, beside the sparkling water of Biscayne Bay, the five of us played a form of baseball Pierre played in his childhood.

Pierre is the permanent pitcher. The rest of us take turns batting. The three who aren't batting play the field and man the bases. We pretend there are "ghost runners" on the bases to bring in the runs. Each batter hits and scores until they have three outs. Whoever gets the highest score wins.

Each boy takes his turn at bat. The "ghost men" run. Pierre makes the close calls. To be sure, there is plenty of arguing.

It is my turn to bat.

"Move in," Trevor yells. "Mom's up."

All three boys move inside the bases. They lean forward, punch their gloves with their fists. I swing the bat a few times to warm up, adjust the brim on my baseball cap, spit for good measure. Then Pierre pitches the ball, and I swing with everything I've got.

When the ball miraculously makes contact with the bat, you can hear the whack all over the park. The ball goes sailing over everyone's head and out of sight, into the mangrove swamp. The boys are so surprised they forget to run after it. They just stand and stare at me.

I smile at them as I round the bases.

"Awesome," I hear one of them say softly.

I have never hit a baseball that well in all my life, nor have I hit one that well since. But on that day in the Miami sunshine with the water of Biscayne Bay shimmering next to us, I show the boys a side of me they don't know about. I disrupt their preconceptions.

It is the same wide-eyed stare I get in the backyard with Lance trying to make me go nuts over his smoking a cigar. Instead, I meet him head-on, take a big drag on it, and send the smoke up into the air, where it lingers in the summer twilight for a long time and lingers still in the photograph I have and in the memories we all treasure.

There is a sense in which once you have had cancer, it never entirely goes away. A small headache immediately brings the thought that it has spread to the brain; a cough means the lungs. I am paranoid, as many patients become, pointing out all my aches and pains to my indulgent doctors. I am told this fear diminishes with time.

Although it can take two years or more to completely overcome the effects of all I have been through, I start to feel like a human being again. At first I notice it in small ways. When I pull into a parking lot, I actually feel like walking from my car to a store, something I haven't felt like doing for months. Dr. Sherbert warns me not to have any sun for a year after chemotherapy, but I can work in the shade planting flowers, and I do a lot of it. I enjoy the pool in the evenings. I take time to read and to write.

I begin running with my friend J. J. Benkert. Several mornings a week we meet on the grounds of the nearby Cranbrook prep school and huff and puff ourselves through the magnificent gardens until we are comfortably running three miles a day. We talk as we run and discover that we think alike on many issues. We find there is no topic we cannot discuss. J. J. becomes the friend I need in Michigan.

My relationship with my mom begins to blossom. When we talk, I hear the love coming through. I don't know how many years we will have left to build our relationship, but I now know that each moment of sharing our love for each other is a gift to be treasured.

My hair grows back in, slowly at first and then fast. I store away my wig, keeping it, since it could come in handy for bad hair days. But I probably won't use it for that. My perspective has changed—just having hair is a good hair day.

Dr. Sherbert works to recreate the nipple of my breast with minor surgery, but with my radiated skin it isn't perfect. Four weeks later, he tattoos the area to complete the illusion of the areola. Overall, my reconstruction turns out so well I can still wear that purple bikini that Pierre likes.

When I step out of the shower in the morning I see the fading scar on my reconstructed breast in the mirror and it reminds me that life can be taken away from us at any moment.

Oddly enough, I find that in many ways I am thankful for the cancer journey. For more than a year I withdrew from normal life and became almost completely unaware of occurrences in the rest of the world. It was my world I was concerned about. Besides the hours I spent at work, I was almost exclusively focused on what happened within my own family and inside my own body. I also spent more than a year watching to see if God would prove Himself to be all that He says He is in the Bible. He did not disappoint me.

Like the boys having their preconceptions of me disrupted, so God disrupted my preconceptions of Him, proving Himself to be so much more than I ever hoped or imagined. And I say this not just because I survived the cancer. If I had died, or if I still die young from a recurrence, I have seen with my own eyes and experienced in my own life that our God is all that we need Him to be. He shows Himself to be mightiest when we are weakest. He brings His peace, a peace that transcends all human understanding, when our lives are turned upside down.

Cancer teaches many lessons, not the least of which is, learn to live one day at a time. We live in a world of five-year plans, Palm Pilots, and increasingly sophisticated retirement accounts. But you won't find those in the Bible. Jesus Himself said,

> "Seek first his kingdom and his righteousness, and all these things [food and clothing] will be given to you as well. Therefore do not worry about tomorrow, for tomorrow will worry about itself. Each day has enough trouble of its own." (Matthew 6:33–34)

God gives us a beautiful illustration of living one day at a time in Exodus 16 after the Israelites have escaped from Egypt. They are in the desert grumbling against Moses and Aaron because they have nothing to eat and are afraid of starving to death. The Lord then rains down bread from heaven, called manna, which the people are to collect; and except for the sixth day, they may collect only what they need for each day. Every day they must accept what God provides, trusting that He will provide again tomorrow.

For a full year I watched carefully to see what God was providing. He was providing plenty, but if I hadn't been looking for Him, I could easily have missed most of it in the commotion of illness, treatments, doctors, and hospitals.

Look for God, for every day you wake up is a gift.

The suffering of cancer is not unlike the suffering of the Old Testament's Job. After he loses everything, Job asks God, "Why?" as he sits among the ashes scraping his sores with a piece of broken pottery. In all, Job asks God why more than a dozen times. Not once does God answer.

It is not until Job stops asking why that God finally speaks. And He lets Job know that it is God himself who will do the questioning:

> *"Who is this that darkens my counsel*
>
> *with words without knowledge?*
>
> *Brace yourself like a man;*
>
> *I will question you,*
>
> *and you shall answer me.*

"Where were you when I laid the earth's foundation?

Tell me, if you understand.

Who marked off its dimensions? Surely you know!"

Job 38:2–5

Job is silent.

God continues with a whole series of questions for Job, which clearly reveal Job's place in relationship to God Himself. "Have you ever given orders to the morning, or shown the dawn its place, that it might take the earth by the edges and shake the wicked out of it?" (vv. 12–13). "What is the way to the abode of light? And where does darkness reside? Can you take them to their places?" (vv. 19–20). "Do you send the lightning bolts on their way? Do they report to you, 'Here we are'?" (v. 35).

There are many more questions. A sober and silent Job knows that God alone is sovereign.

While the Bible is clear that God is not usually the cause of suffering (we can blame Satan and ourselves for most of it), He allows our suffering and often uses it to make us better. Why? Sometimes because time is short, and suffering is the fastest way to get us where God needs us to be. In Job's case, God takes a good man and allows him to see his Father in heaven through new eyes.

In my case, a similar change in vision has occurred.

This I know: In suffering we receive the unique privilege of experiencing fellowship with Christ in His suffering, without which, and even in many ways with which, we cannot begin to understand the power of His resurrection. Next to Job, perhaps no individual has ever suffered more than the apostle Paul, yet he embraced suffering, writing:

I want to know Christ and the power of his resurrection and the fellowship of sharing in his sufferings, becoming like him in his death, and so, somehow, to attain to the resurrection from the dead. (Philippians 3:10–11)

He gives us several accounts of the hardships he endured for the mission of spreading the good news of Jesus Christ. In one of these accounts Paul says:

> Three times I was beaten with rods, once I was stoned, three times I was shipwrecked, I spent a night and a day in the open sea, I have been constantly on the move. I have been in danger from rivers, in danger from bandits, in danger from my own countrymen, in danger from Gentiles; in danger in the city, in danger in the country, in danger at sea; and in danger from false brothers. I have labored and toiled and have often gone without sleep; I have known hunger and thirst and have often gone without food; I have been cold and naked. (2 Corinthians 11:25–27)

Yet Paul keeps going, keeps spreading the good news, for although he is all too familiar with suffering, Paul also knows intimately the promise of the Resurrection. He knows there is more to come, and he knows it because he has personally had a look, having been "caught up to the third heaven. . . . up to paradise. He heard inexpressible things, things that man is not permitted to tell" (2 Corinthians 12:2, 4).

No eye has seen,

no ear has heard,

no mind has conceived

what God has prepared for those who love him.

1 Corinthians 2:9

Suffering may never make sense in this life. It is for this future paradise that our suffering somehow prepares us, for the day when we are at last completely transformed into the likeness of Christ and ushered into the presence of "the King of kings and Lord of lords, who alone is immortal and who lives in unapproachable light" (1 Timothy 6:15–16).

X X X

I have a second dream of a tidal wave. This dream is different than the first in which I woke up just before the water came thundering over me. In this second dream, I am a passenger in a car driving along a beach that is crescent-shaped. Through the windshield I see a row of houses standing along the beachfront. The sea sparkles in the sunlight. Gentle waves lap the shoreline. There is one house covered in well-weathered brown shingles that particularly catches my eye. I don't know who is driving the car, but we stop to look.

Suddenly, as in the first dream, I see a towering tidal wave that rears up ominously and approaches fast. This time, however, I see the scene from inside the shelter of the car and at a distance. I am an observer as the water thunders over the houses and then recedes. Although other houses crumble, the house that I watch stands firm against the onslaught of water.

Jesus said:

> "I will show you what he is like who comes to me and hears my words and puts them into practice. He is like a man building a house, who dug down deep and laid the foundation on rock. When a flood came, the torrent struck that house but could not shake it, because it was well built." (Luke 6:47–48)

Since I was twenty-two years old, I have built my life with Christ as my foundation, and when cancer came I bet my life on Him. He held me fast.

The seas have lifted up, O LORD,

the seas have lifted up their voice;

the seas have lifted up their pounding waves.

Mightier than the thunder of the great waters,

mightier than the breakers of the sea—

the LORD on high is mighty.

Psalm 93:3–4

JOURNEY SURVIVAL GUIDE

In cancer, or any life crisis, the most important thing to do is to be certain that you have received God's free gift of salvation through Jesus Christ. With that assurance, you are God's child and He takes responsibility for everything that happens to you. So live one day at a time. Spend your life. Use it up. Don't wait until things settle down to do the things you really care about. Seize the opportunities that present themselves, no matter what the circumstances. Don't let your suffering be wasted. Serve the Lord now. Tomorrow is not guaranteed for any of us. And always remember, the Lord says:

"I will not forget you!
    See, I have engraved you on the
palms of my hands."
Isaiah 49:15–16

JOURNEY RESOURCES

The Bible. God's Word is your most important book. No matter what else you are reading, try to spend time in your Bible every day to find courage through difficult times, hope for healing, and to stay focused on your ultimate goal, Jesus.

Your Doctors. You and your doctors are a team. Write down questions before your appointments. Good doctors will take the time to answer them to your satisfaction. If your doctor is in too much of a hurry or is condescending, consider a change. There are many fine doctors out there. You are fighting for your life.

The American Cancer Society. Call your local chapter, call 1-800-ACS-2345, or visit their Web site, cancer.org, for information regarding all kinds of cancer, treatments, prevention, publications, support groups, and more.

National Cancer Institute. Visit the Web site at <u>nationalcancerin-stitute.com</u> to learn more about cancer and its treatment, personal stories, research, support, e-mail groups, and more. Or call their Cancer Information Service at 1-800-4-CANCER.

Barbara Ann Karmanos Cancer Institute. Karmanos is affiliated with The Detroit Medical Center and Wayne State University. This is one of the easiest Web sites to navigate at <u>Karmanos.org</u>, featuring articles about topics of interest and current trials. Or call 1-800-KARMANOS to speak to a staff member. Be sure to ask for their free newsletter, *Answers to Cancer.*

The Word on Health: A Biblical and Medical Overview of How to Care for Your Body and Mind (Chicago: Moody, 2000), by Dr. Michael D. Jacobson. The title says it all. This book offers principles for achieving optimal health through nutrition and lifestyle provided by our Creator Himself. Chapter 2, "The Word on Why People Get Sick," offers unique insight for cancer patients.

Dr. Susan Love's Breast Book, 2d ed. (New York: Penguin, 2000), by Susan M. Love, M.D. This comprehensive book is a kind of encyclopedia of information about every aspect of the breast, including breast cancer. Nearly every term your doctor uses is defined, and treatments are described in clinical detail. However, check the publication date. Survival statistics are improving every year.

Cancer: 50 Essential Things to Do (New York: NAL, 1999), by Greg Anderson. Written by a survivor who defied the doctors that sent him home to die, this book describes what cancer survivors have in common. It provides practical tips so that you can fight cancer on every level, including physical, mental, emotional, and nutritional. Unfortunately, the author's discussion of the importance of "the spiritual" life in healing is not based on God's Word, so use it along with your Bible.

Minding the Body, Mending the Mind (New York: Simon & Schuster, 1988; also New York: Bantam, 1988), by Joan Borysenko. This is another resource that should be used in tandem with your Bible. Many patients find the relaxation techniques very helpful for enduring the realities of cancer, its treatments, and side effects.

Food—Your Miracle Medicine: Preventing and Curing Common Health Problems the Natural Way (New York: Harper Collins, 1998; also Harper Paperbacks, 1993), by Jean Carper. This easy reference helps you make dietary changes so you can use food to promote healing.

Living Beyond Breast Cancer: A Survivor's Guide for When Treatment Ends and the Rest of Your Life Begins (Collingdale, Pa.: DIANE, 2000; also paperback by Times Books/Random House, 1997), by Marisa C. Weiss, M.D., and Ellen Weiss. Get back to a "normal" life with this helpful resource dealing with managing post-treatment problems such as fears of recurrence, reentering the job market, feelings of unattractiveness, and sexual drive.

Survivors. Others who have been on the cancer journey can be a tremendous help if they have a positive attitude. If someone offers to come alongside you, consider letting her.

The Local Church. If you are not affiliated with a local church offering sound doctrine and people who minister to one another, this is the time to find one. God uses the church to work on His behalf. His people become His hands to serve and help us in our time of need.

Our Mighty God. Clearly our Lord is our greatest resource. If you are tempted to turn away in anger and bitterness, make a sharp U-turn back into His presence. No matter what the outcome of your individual circumstances, He promises to uphold you every step of the way. Watch for Him. He is faithful.

A WOMAN'S GUIDE TO BREAST CARE

The early detection of breast cancer is critical. The American Cancer Society has published "Recommendations for the Early Detection of Breast Cancer" and "Increased Risk for Breast Cancer." These materials are given below (Reprinted by the permission of the American Cancer Society, Inc.).

American Cancer Society Recommendations for the Early Detection of Breast Cancer

Women aged 40 and older should have a screening mammogram every year.

Between the ages of 20 and 39, women should have a clinical breast examination by a health professional every 3 years.

After age 40, women should have a breast exam by a health professional every year.

Women aged 20 or older should perform breast self-examination (BSE) every month. By doing the exam regularly, you get to know how your breasts normally feel and you can more readily detect any change. If a change occurs, such as development of a lump or swelling in the breast or underarm area, skin irritation or dimpling, nipple pain or retraction (turning inward), redness or scaliness of the nipple or breast skin, or a discharge other than breast milk, you should see your health care provider as soon as possible for evaluation. However, remember that most of the time, these breast changes are not cancer.

Increased Risk for Breast Cancer

Your risk of developing breast cancer increases with age. About 77% of women with breast cancer are older than 50 when they are diagnosed.

Women with first-degree relatives with breast cancer on either the mother's or [the] father's side of the family have a higher breast cancer risk.

Women who have had no children or who had their first child after age 30 have a slightly higher breast cancer risk.

A woman with cancer in one breast has a 3- to 4-fold increased risk of developing a new cancer in the other breast or in another part of the same breast.

Women who are overweight.

Monthly Breast Self-Exam

As the American Cancer Society recommendations indicate, every woman aged twenty and over should conduct breast self-examination (BSE) each month. You should do this exam seven to ten days after your period begins, or, if you have reached menopause, on the first day of the month. The following steps are ones you can follow as you do this exam.

Step 1

In the shower. Stand in the shower and with your fingers flat (do not use the tips of your fingers) move your hand gently over every part of each breast. Check for a lump, knot, or thickening. Use your right hand for your left breast, your left hand for your right breast.

Step 2

Before a mirror. With your hands at your sides, visually check for lumps or depressions (hollows). Then, placing your palms on your hips, press down firmly, flex your chest muscles, and check again. Don't worry if your breasts don't match—chances are they will be a little different.

Step 3

Before a mirror. Now raise your arms overhead. Look for changes in the contours of each breast as well as any swelling, dimpling of the skin, or changes in the nipple.

Step 4

Lying down. To examine your right breast, place a pillow or folded towel under your right shoulder and put your right arm behind your head. Move your left hand in a circular, up and down line, or wedge pattern all around the breast. Then place the pillow under your left shoulder and your left hand behind your head, and examine your left breast in the same manner, using your right hand.

Step 5

Lying down. With your fingers flat, use your left hand to press an imaginary clock face (a circle) on your right breast. Check for lumps or depressions (hollows). A ridge of firm tissue in the lower curve is normal. Move in an inch toward the nipple and make the same circling motion again and again until you reach the center. Repeat with your right hand, left breast. (Be sure to press firmly.)

Step 6

Lying down. Gently squeeze the nipple of each breast. Check for any discharge. Report any lumps, thickenings, or discharges you discover during the examination to your doctor immediately.

If you are interested in information about other books written from a biblical perspective, please write to the following address:
Northfield Publishing
215 West Locust Street
Chicago, IL 60610